FORGOTTEN VOICES OF THE SECOND WORLD WAR

FORGOTTEN VOICES OF THE SECOND WORLD WAR

IN ASSOCIATION WITH THE

IMPERIAL WAR MUSEUM

MAX ARTHUR

EBURY PRESS
LONDON

1 3 5 7 9 10 8 6 4 2

Published in 2007 by Ebury Press, an imprint of Ebury Publishing

A Random House Group Company

The Random House Group Limited Reg. No. 954009

Addresses for companies within the Random House Group can be found atwww.randomhouse.co.uk

A CIP catalogue record for this book is available from the British Library.

The Random House Group Limited makes every effort to ensure that the papers used in our books are made from trees that have been legally sourced from well-managed and credibly certified forests. Our paper procurement policy can be found on www.randomhouse.co.uk

To buy books by your favourite authors and register for offers visit www.rbooks.co.uk

Editor: Amanda Li
Designer: David Fordham

ISBN 9780091917746

Printed and bound in Singapore by Tien Wah Press

PAGE 2: *A sailor on watch, wearing a duffle coat, steel helmet and binoculars. A pom-pom gun is in the foreground.*

NOTE: Some of the following accounts contain weights and measurements in the Imperial system, which was in use at the time of the Second World War. Here is a conversion table showing the approximate metric equivalents.

DISTANCE
1 inch = 2.5 centimetres
1 foot = 30 centimetres
1 yard = 0.9 metres
1 mile = 1.6 kilometres

WEIGHT
1 pound (abbreviated as 'lb') = 0.4 kilogrammes
1 hundredweight = 50 kilogrammes

ABOVE: *This poster shows a German Zeppelin flying above the London skyline to emphasise the danger of bombing in England and encourage volunteers to join the Army.*

CONTENTS

1 PRELUDE TO WAR

WAR TALK   28
People's feelings about the impending war

LEAVING THE CITY   34
Evacuees and their families tell their stories

2 FIGHTING THE WAR

THE GERMAN INVASION   42
Soldiers and civilians describe their experiences
of the *Blitzkrieg*

BATTLE IN THE AIR   57
How the Battle of Britain was fought

THE BLITZ   65
Living through the bombing of British cities

WAR AT SEA   71
Accounts from the Battle of the Atlantic

ACTION IN THE DESERT   77
How soldiers fought in the Western Desert

WAR IN THE MEDITERRANEAN   84
The invasion of Crete and the siege of Malta

ACKNOWLEDGEMENTS

I WISH TO THANK Christopher Dowling, the former Director of Public Services at the Imperial War Museum, who originally offered me this challenging project and gave me wholehearted support. Within the Imperial War Museum I am indebted to Margaret Brooks, the Keeper of the Sound Archive, and her excellent staff. I must also thank the Imperial War Museum's historian Terry Charman for his valuable contribution to the book, and Liz Bowers for all her help.

At my publishers Ebury Press I owe a debt to Carey Smith, my editor, who has been a tower of strength. My agent, Barbara Levy, who is also the agent for the Imperial War Museum, helped create the project and has been a hundred per cent behind it throughout and I thank her.

PREFACE
to the Original Edition

Forgotten Voices of the Second World War is a sequel to *Forgotten Voices of the Great War* and has been created from the remarkable collection of taped interviews held by the Sound Archive of the Imperial War Museum. It is an archive of extraordinary depth, containing thousands of taped recordings of men and women who have served or witnessed the wars and campaigns from the First World War to the present.

The Second World War archive contains several thousand taped interviews recorded over the last thirty years. I have drawn extensively from this archive and listened to hundreds of hours of tapes and read countless transcripts of people's experiences of war.

Apart from a number of French and German accounts, the Imperial War Museum interviews primarily cover British and Commonwealth participants, so I have concentrated on the campaigns where they have been involved. The exception is the Salerno landings, where the personal accounts are of American troops. These accounts come from a collection presented to the Sound Archive some years ago.

What I have sought to do is capture the experiences and atmosphere of the Second World War: the waiting, the preparation, the action and the consequences of those actions. Some of these accounts are raw and horrific, others more matter-of-fact or reflective. They all have their place in the tapestry of war.

Max Arthur

Wait!
Count 15
slowly
before moving in the Blackout
g.r. morris
Issued by THE NATIONAL "SAFETY FIRST" ASSOCIATION (Inc.), Terminal House, 52, Grosvenor Gardens, London, S.W. 1

About the
Second World
War

'I remember vividly "peace in our time" –
Neville Chamberlain coming back from
Munich. We thought, "Thank God, it's going
to be peace. It's not going to be war."
But of course, events proved wrong.'

Evelyn White, Civilian in Birmingham

The Second World War (1939-45) was the most destructive and widespread conflict the world has ever seen. It involved more countries and even larger numbers of people than the devastating First World War. Huge numbers of civilians – ordinary men, women and children – were affected and millions died, both in battle and on the home front, during the six years that the war raged.

Left: *A poster calling for everyone to be cautious and think carefully before moving in a blackout.*

The Second World War has been described as a 'total war', as it took up all the resources, both human and material, of the nations involved. Every major world power became involved and fighting took place on land, at sea and in the air, from Europe and Asia to Africa and the islands of the Pacific. When hostilities finally came to an end, many countries were left on the verge of collapse.

THE ROAD TO WAR

THE WAR BEGAN IN TWO DIFFERENT REGIONS OF THE WORLD AT DIFFERENT times – in the Far East and in Europe.

In the Far East, Japan had been making plans to expand her empire into South-East Asia and the islands of the South-West Pacific. Defying the League of Nations, Japanese troops invaded the Chinese province of Manchuria in 1931. In 1937, following an incident between Japanese and Chinese soldiers outside Peking at the

THE EXTENT OF THE HOSTILITIES ACROSS THE WORLD

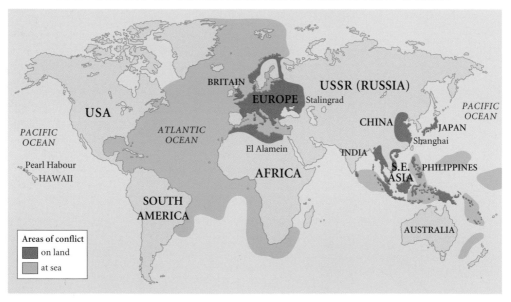

ABOVE: *Map showing the widespread areas of fighting on land and at sea across the world.*

WHY DID THE SECOND WORLD WAR HAPPEN?

Like the First World War, the long-term causes of this conflict were complex.

Throughout the 1930s there was a worldwide economic slump, which led to poor social conditions and political instability in many countries. In this difficult climate, extreme political movements, most notably Fascism, prospered and grew, and extremist leaders such as Hitler in Germany, Mussolini in Italy and Stalin, the Communist leader of The Soviet Union adopted aggressive foreign policies.

In an effort to keep the peace following the First World War, the victorious nations had formed The League of Nations, an organisation whose aim was to discuss international disputes and act as peacekeeper in the event of any future aggression by one nation against another. The League was not successful. The most powerful nation and defender of democracy at that time, the USA, was not even a member. Other major nations such as Germany and the Soviet Union, who became members in later years, had little or no influence. In the end, the League of Nations did not have the power to enforce the decisions it made.

The Treaty of Versailles was drawn up in 1919 to establish peace terms and to reorganise Europe in its post-war upheaval. The terms, however, were harsh on the defeated Germany – all her overseas colonies were seized, territory in Europe was taken away, her military forces were limited and millions of pounds in compensation had to be paid for war damage. There was much bitterness amongst the poverty-stricken German people, who saw themselves as being unnecessarily punished for their part in the war. The 1930s saw the rise of the leader, Adolf Hitler, and his National Socialist party (the Nazis) who were to become the most powerful political party in Germany. In January 1933 Hitler became Chancellor (Prime Minister) and democracy effectively came to an end in Germany.

Marco Polo bridge, Japan launched an invasion of China. Fighting had been going on for two years by the time war broke out in Europe but it soon became part of the global conflict. Japan joined forces with Germany and Italy in 1940.

In Europe, Hitler broke the terms of the Treaty of Versailles in 1936 when he sent German troops into the Rhineland, an area where Germany was no longer allowed to have military forces. The Germans went on to occupy Austria in March 1938, declaring a union between the two countries. Hitler then turned his attention to Czechoslovakia and the situation became critical. Anxious to avoid war, the British Prime Minister, Neville Chamberlain, flew to Germany for talks with the German, French and Italian leaders. The outcome was the controversial Munich agreement, which allowed the Germans to take over the disputed Sudetenland area of Czechoslovakia; in return, Hitler stated that he would demand no further land in Europe. A delighted Chamberlain returned home promising 'Peace in our time'. Six months later, German forces seized the rest of Czechoslovakia.

ABOVE: *Neville Chamberlain makes a brief speech announcing 'Peace in our Time' on his return from meeting Hitler in Munich.*

ABOVE: *German troops pouring through the gates into Prague as the German army advances further into Europe.*

Realising that Hitler could not be trusted, the Allies began to prepare for war. Poland was the next target for Hitler, who was anxious to reclaim an area of land known as the Polish Corridor. Britain and France made an alliance with Poland that stated that in the event of a German invasion, both countries would defend the Poles. In August 1939 the Germans and the Soviets made their own agreement, in which plans were made to invade Poland and divide her territory between them. Germany invaded on 1 September. On 3 September Britain and France declared war on Germany.

A SHORT HISTORY OF THE WAR

THE MAJOR ALLIED POWERS	THE MAJOR AXIS POWERS
BRITAIN FRANCE USA (after 7 December 1941 – Pearl Harbor) **THE SOVIET UNION** (after 22 June 1941 – when Hitler invaded the Soviet Union) CHINA	GERMANY ITALY JAPAN (after 7 December 1941 – Pearl Harbor) ROMANIA

1939

FOLLOWING THE OCCUPATION OF CZECHOSLOVAKIA, THE GERMANS INVADED Poland on 1 September. Having promised to guarantee Polish independence, Britain and France declared war two days later. Preparations for war were made but at first there were no signs of fighting in western Europe.

WHAT WAS THE 'PHONEY WAR'?

The first few months following the September declaration of war were eerily quiet and this period became known as the 'Phoney War'. British and French forces were mobilized and remained on the defensive in Europe as Christmas came. Many evacuees returned to their families during this time, as people could see no evidence of a war starting.

Following the pact made with the Germans, Soviet Union troops followed Germany into Poland on 17 September and the two countries signed a treaty which divided Poland up between them. The Soviet Union then invaded Finland.

Conflict began in the Atlantic Ocean soon after war was declared as the Allies desperately needed to keep their shipping lanes open for essential supplies. Packs of German U-boat submarines gathered in the Atlantic and inflicted severe losses on Allied convoys throughout the war, in what is known as the Battle of the Atlantic.

1940

THE GERMANS LAUNCHED A SUDDEN SWEEPING ASSAULT OF *BLITZKRIEG* – 'lightning war' - across Western Europe between April and May, attacking first Denmark and Norway, then Holland, France and Belgium. The British Expeditionary Force (BEF) fought a rearguard action back to the beaches of Dunkirk, where over 338,000 Allied troops were evacuated to England. The Prime Minister, Neville Chamberlain, resigned and was replaced by Winston Churchill.

ABOVE: *Prime Minister Winston Churchill in naval dress for a visit to the SS Queen Mary in America.*

Wanting to strike while Britain's armed forces were still in disarray, Hitler needed air superiority over the Channel to launch an invasion of Britain. The German air force – the Luftwaffe – began its attack in July and the Battle of Britain took place in the skies above southern England. Despite heavy losses of men and aircraft on both sides, the Luftwaffe were defeated by the RAF in October. On 7 September they began bombing Britain's cities (the Blitz) to destroy production and terrorise the civilian population.

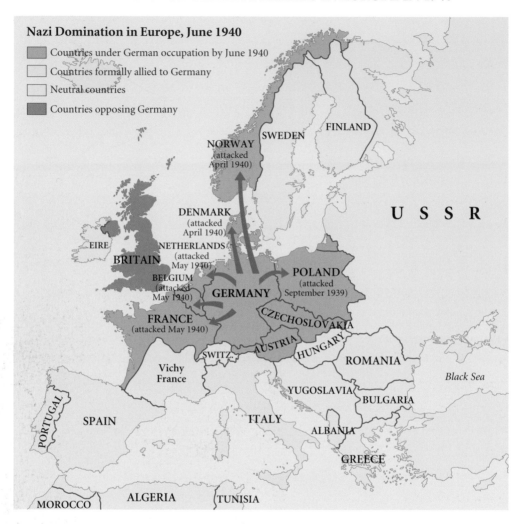

Italy declared war on Britain and France on 10 June. Across Europe, and around the Mediterranean, the Axis alliance of Germany and Italy launched actions to protect their supply routes from Africa to mainland Europe. In June, Italian bombers attacked Malta and in September Italian troops entered Egypt from Libya. In October they invaded Greece, effectively opening up two new fronts. British air force units were sent to the defence of Greece, landing on 2 November. In early December the British attacked the Italians in the deserts of western Egypt.

1941

IN JANUARY ALLIED TROOPS CAPTURED TOBRUK IN LIBYA AND DEFEATED ITALIAN forces in the Western Desert in February. Germany sent in the Afrika Korps and fierce fighting took place, but the Allies managed to hold out against them.

In April, in the Mediterranean, British forces were ordered to evacuate Greece and make their way to Crete, where German troops were parachuted in on 20 May. Despite huge losses, the Germans drove the British off the island and a fierce battle began to keep supply lines open to the then British colony of Malta and to prevent the island from being invaded.

Having failed to invade Britain, Hitler turned his attention to the Soviet Union. On 22 June *Operation Barbarossa* was launched, an invasion plan to conquer Russia. In September Leningrad (St Petersburg) came under siege when German and Finnish troops surrounded the entire city.

The war in the Atlantic continued with huge losses for British shipping, however, the sinking of the Bismarck by British fleets came as a blow for the German navy.

As 1941 drew to a close, the final major nations entered the war. On 7 December, Japanese dive-bombers simultaneously attacked the US fleet at Pearl

ABOVE: *The USS Pennsylvania, the United States Fleet Flagship, and two wrecked destroyers after the surprise Japanese attack on Pearl Harbour.*

Harbor, Hawaii, and British bases in Malaya and Hong Kong. Four days later, Hitler declared war on the United States. America declared war in return – her massive resources and military might were now joined to the Allied war effort. The Japanese turned immediately to the American military bases on the Philippines and continued their assault in Malaya. Taken by surprise by the speed of the Japanese attacks, Hong Kong surrendered.

On the Eastern Front, the Soviet Union made a successful counter-offensive in early December, thus removing the threat to Moscow.

1942

AT THE START OF THE YEAR THE AXIS POWERS MADE ADVANCES, WITH THE exception of the Eastern Front. Rommel launched a major offensive in North Africa while the Japanese, having seized Singapore and Malaya, surged on through the Pacific taking Borneo, Java, New Guinea and Burma. The remaining British troops in Burma retreated, leaving the Japanese in control.

In June, the US fleet defeated Japanese naval forces in the Battle of Midway, which was regarded as a turning point in the war as it prevented the Japanese gaining naval supremacy in the Pacific.

German troops resumed their advance to the Soviet city of Stalingrad in August. The Battle of Stalingrad, which took place during the winter months of 1942-43, saw some of the most brutal fighting of the war. The eventual defeat of the German troops was a disaster for Hitler, who lost many thousands of men.

Montgomery took command of the Eighth Army in the Western Desert in August, and inflicted heavy losses on the Afrika Korps. By the end of the year, following the second battle of El Alamein, he had retaken Tobruk, and the Germans were in retreat.

As the year continued, Australian troops finally halted the Japanese drive through New Guinea and British troops re-entered Burma to resume the fight at Arakan.

The Allies stepped up their bombing of Germany and in May the first contingents of the United States Army Air Force (USAAF) arrived in England.

1943

THIS WAS A YEAR OF PUSHING BACK THE TIDE OF AXIS ADVANCES. IN THE Soviet Union the Germans began to withdraw from the Caucasus region in January. In February the last German resistance was crushed in Stalingrad and Soviet forces began to march towards Poland. In the same month the first of the 'Chindit' campaigns began against the Japanese in Burma.

The round-the-clock Allied bombing of Germany continued and on 16 May the famous 'Dambusters' raid was carried out, using the newly developed bouncing bomb. Further raids brought devastation to German civilians, as well as heavy casualties among Allied aircrew and planes.

Allied victory in North Africa enabled an invasion of Italy to be launched. Following landings on the island of Sicily, Allied troops landed at Salerno on the

ABOVE: *Russian soldiers hoist the Red Flag over a recaptured factory during the battle of Stalingrad.*

ABOVE: *A low-level aerial photograph of the devastated city centre of Stuttgart from the south-west, after 53 major raids, most of them by Bomber Command, destroyed nearly 68 percent of its built-up area and killed 4,562 people.*

mainland, meeting heavy German opposition as they fought northwards to Rome. Italy surrendered in September and declared war on Germany in October.

In the Atlantic, the tide was turning. The U-boat packs had sunk 120 Allied ships in March and, to counter-attack, the Allies sent support groups of warships and air assistance to protect their convoys. Soon, U-boats were sunk in significant numbers and were forced to withdraw to safer waters.

1944

OVERSTRETCHED ON TWO FRONTS – IN THE SOVIET UNION AND ITALY, WHERE Rome finally fell on 4 June – Germany was struggling to survive.

The stage was set by June for the Allies to launch an invasion of Europe to liberate France – D-Day. The troops had been trained and prepared, planners had put the final touches to the invasion scheme, and members of the Resistance in France and the Special Operations Executive had prepared a programme of sabotage to support the landings. D-Day began the fight-back in North-Western Europe, and with Allied troops landed in the South of France and pressing north, the German Army found itself in an impossible position. On 25 August Paris was liberated.

Months of fighting followed and by mid-December Allied troops had reached the forests of the Ardennes in northern France. Here, German forces carried out a determined last-ditch attack on American forces known as 'The Battle of the Bulge'.

In the Pacific, American land, air and sea forces carried out an island-hopping campaign against Japanese troops, effectively destroying the Japanese fleet at Leyte Gulf in October. In Burma the British Fourteenth Army halted an attempted Japanese invasion of India at the Indian towns of Imphal and Kohima.

1945

AT THE BEGINNING OF THE YEAR GERMANY WAS UNDER INVASION, ALLIED forces were advancing towards Berlin, and the end of the conflict in Europe was only a matter of time. On the night of 13/14 February the city of Dresden was destroyed by Allied bombers and many thousands of civilians were killed in the resulting firestorms. The bombing has remained controversial.

By April Berlin was surrounded by Soviet troops and it was here that Hitler committed suicide. On 7 May, Germany surrendered. The following day, thousands of people in Britain and France celebrated the Allied victory in Europe.

However, in the Far East, fighting went on for another three months. Although the British had largely secured Burma by spring, there was still strong Japanese resistance in the Pacific islands. American president Harry Truman decided to bring about a swift end to the war and ordered the first ever atomic bomb to be used. On 6 August an American bomber released the bomb over the Japanese city of Hiroshima, killing many thousands of people. Three days later, a second bomb was dropped on Nagasaki. The Japanese surrendered on 14 August. The war was over.

THE CONSEQUENCES OF THE WAR

THE SECOND WORLD WAR BROUGHT DEATH AND DESTRUCTION ON A GREATER scale than any war before it. Whole cities were destroyed and vast areas of land decimated. No one knows exactly how many people were killed – it is estimated to be 55 million – but it is known that even more civilians died than soldiers.

LEFT: *A barrage balloon, near Biggin Hill, Kent. Large numbers of barrage balloons were located across the south-eastern approaches to London to combat the growing threat from V-1 flying bombs.*

How the Second World War Shaped the Modern World

The reconstruction of many countries after the war was a slow and painful proooce. The world was re-defined politically and Germany was split into two countries, East and West, divided by the Berlin Wall in 1961. Today Germany is one country again. The US and the Soviet Union had been allies during the war but their relationship deteriorated in the following years. A new kind of war emerged – The Cold War, characterised by a build up of nuclear arms and years of tension between the US and the Soviet Union, who were now the two world superpowers. This conflict continued until the early 1990s.

In 1945 the United Nations was established, with 50 member nations signing up to its charter. The object was to maintain world peace and develop relationships between nations. The UN plays a vital role as peace keeper in the world today.

One of the more shocking discoveries of the war was the human cost of Nazi ideology. In Hitler's Germany many groups of people, including Jews, Romanies and the physically and mentally disabled, were regarded as inferior to the Nazi ideal of the physically perfect Aryan (white, Nordic race). At the end of the war it was discovered that six million Jewish people had been murdered or had died in concentration camps – this act of mass murder was named the Holocaust. Following the war, Jewish nationalists campaigned for large areas of Palestine to become Israel – the Jewish homeland. This was agreed by the United Nations in 1948 and Palestine was divided into a Jewish and an Arab state.

Many technological advances were made during the war, including the development of the computer and of radar systems. However, the one advance that has had the single most impact on the modern world was the harnessing of atomic energy, which led to the development of the world's first atomic bomb. The bomb was first used by the Americans against the Japanese in 1945, with devastating results.

ABOVE: *The mushroom cloud over Nagasaki after the atomic bomb had been dropped.*

1

PRELUDE
TO
WAR

LEFT: *A woman war worker machining pistons
for a Rolls Royce aero engine.*
ABOVE: *A Girl Guide and a Sea Ranger selling saving stamps.*

WAR TALK

Young men joined up, many before conscription reached them – and women too embraced a new life in the forces. Those who remembered the First World War, however, saw bleak times ahead.

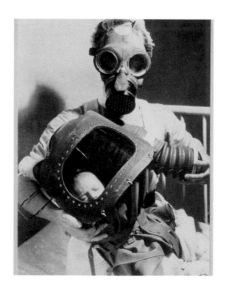

BELOW LEFT: *Fully kitted out to face a gas attack, a nurse shows how to fit a special baby's gas mask.*

RIGHT: *A newspaper seller with the announcement of the official declaration of war.*

Evelyn White
Civilian in Birmingham

I BEGAN THINKING, 'IS IT GOING TO BE LIKE THE FIRST WORLD WAR?' when thousands of men were killed. In a way, they were human fodder. I thought, 'Is it going to be a repeat? What's going to happen to my brothers?'

Dorothy Williams
Teenager at outbreak of war

IT WAS A VERY ANXIOUS TIME. MY PARENTS FOLLOWED THE EVENTS VERY closely, so when we knew that war could break out – I think it was 11 o'clock in the morning – we were really keyed up. I was frightened. We didn't know what was ahead. We had relatives who had been badly gassed. Father said if the

> *Father said if the Germans ever landed, he would kill us all rather than us ever fall into their hands.*

Germans ever landed, he would kill us all rather than us ever fall into their hands. That frightened us a little bit too – we didn't know which was going to be the worse of the two. Oh yes, he meant it. He had been right through the previous war and he had seen a lot.

We had to go to a hall in the village and collect our gas masks. I never found mine very comfortable. For babies there were the big gas masks in which the child lay. I know my baby sister was absolutely terrified of it. I don't know what would have happened if she had remained in it for a long time because she was so frightened. She screamed the place down and went quite blue in the face. Of course we had to carry them everywhere we went in those little cardboard boxes with a piece of string attached. We never moved without them. **,**

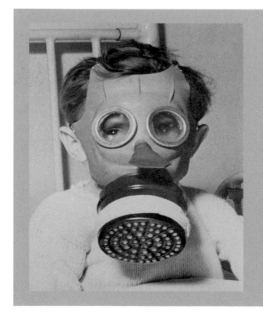

THE THREAT OF GAS

Gas had proved a deadly weapon in the trenches of the First World War and there was now a strong possibility that gas bombs might be dropped on British towns and cities. Gas masks were issued to every person in Britain, including a child's version which featured large eyes and a nose piece and was nicknamed the 'Mickey Mouse'. The masks had to be carried around at all times. However, in the end, gas was not used by Germans against Britain.

LEFT: *Child's ('Mickey Mouse') gas mask which had red rubber face pieces and bright eye-piece rims.*

Jutta Buder
Jewish girl living in Germany

WE WERE ON VACATION IN SEPTEMBER 1939 AND WE WERE PLAYING ON the beach – and our parents came running down to the beach and told us war had broken out, and that we had to go home immediately. I thought it was very exciting, even though I didn't want to leave the beach – and we all pushed into trains and everybody had to go home.

Lieutenant Dick Caldwell
Lieutenant-surgeon, Royal Navy

AS WAR APPROACHED, I THINK THE THOUGHT OF GOING TO WAR WAS exciting. The day war was declared, the admiral called us together in the wardroom and gave us champagne and gave us a toast – 'Damnation to Hitler'.

Henry Metelmann
German youth apprenticed to the railway

GERMANY HAD INVADED POLAND, AND TO US IT WAS SOMETHING GREAT. With shame I express this feeling now, because I had no idea what it really meant to the people there, to be invaded by a foreign army – and anyway, to be honest, I didn't care. I thought of the German greatness and I thought, 'Well, anyway, the Poles are second-rate and they have treated our German people living there very badly. It serves them right.' And also, to think that Germany now could occupy Poland, then surely we would be a powerful state in central Europe – that appealed to me.

People in general did not like it, because many of the neighbours, they remembered the First World War. My father had been a soldier. He said, 'I remember at first it was all great, the colours and all this and fighting for the Kaiser and the Empire. But then later on, things turned and changed, and it could well happen again, because it could be a long war.'

Aircraftwoman Elsie Bartlett
An early recruit to the WAAF

ALL TYPES TURNED UP AT HALLAM STREET TO ENLIST – SHORT, FAT, THIN, small, dowdy, glamorous – typists and shop-girls, married and single, from all walks of life. They were fussy about who they took at the beginning, and I hadn't a lot going for me – what with spinal curvature and bad eyes. However, I slipped in as a grade C3 and, by that evening, was in Harrogate with the King's shilling and a sore arm from injections.

WOMEN IN THE AIR FORCE

The Women's Auxiliary Air Force (WAAF) was formed in June 1939 when war seemed likely. The many and varied jobs that the women undertook were intended to release men for front-line duties in the Royal Air Force. Throughout the war WAAF members worked as clerks, drivers, telephonists, mechanics, aeroplane fitters and in many other roles. The work they did was essential to the war, and in particular during the Battle of Britain.

LEFT: *WAAF plotters move squadron markers around a table map.*

OPPORTUNITIES NOW IN LOCAL FACTORY FOR MARRIED WOMEN TO VOLUNTEER TO FILL THE MILLIONS OF SHELLS NEEDED TO WIN THE WAR

Full details at Employment Exchange

LEAVING THE CITY

When war was declared, thousands of children living in cities and towns were evacuated to safer areas, mostly to the countryside. While many mothers accompanied their children, most adults had to stay behind.

'W<small>E WAVED GOODBYE. T</small>HE PARENTS STAYED ON ONE SIDE OF THE ROAD and they all cried their eyes out – it was terrible, but we were all happy and joking by then. We'd had our apple, bagged our gasmask and we'd said our goodbyes.

We got into Vauxhall Station, and it was like entering a tomb – all tiled and dark. We had to wait down there until the train came in. It was a Southern Railway train that went round the loop line to Reading.

It really was packed! What I remember is the noise – ten carriages of children, and half of them were hanging out the windows. A lot of police there. It was just bedlam. I felt the teachers were very, very harassed, and in retrospect, they did a marvellous

A<small>BOVE</small>: *A group of evacuees arrive at Brent station. About 175 children were evacuated together from Bristol to Devon.*
L<small>EFT</small>: *Homeless children after their houses were destroyed by German air raids.*

Mum said that after we left it was like a cathedral, it was so quiet, the whole area.

job. They shepherded us all there, looked after us – and they were worried themselves – some of their own children were with us.

Mum said that after we left it was like a cathedral, it was so quiet, the whole area. In the evenings, she said, it was unbelievable. They didn't realise 'til then the noise of children playing. The streets had been our playgrounds.

On the train we were all happy – thrilled, adventurous. We whizzed under funny old archways at Clapham Junction and Wandsworth Town; we could see people lined up above it all, waving to us, and that cheered us up no end. We were

ABOVE: *Labelled like parcels, bewildered London evacuees prepare to board a train, which will take them to unfamiliar homes and foster parents. It is unsurprising that many were unhappy.*

joyful for them. We went through Richmond, across the Thames, and you knew we were in the countryside. It wasn't long before we saw cows – we were thrilled. It was a tremendous adventure for us.

When we got to Reading we were taken into a big hall. People came in and sat at desks, then they walked down the line and tried to take pairs and families. I was taken by a local council man. The house was super. We went by car – I just couldn't believe it. My sister and I were just earmarked. 'We wanted a boy and a girl. You'll do.'

We were handed over to a maid. We hardly saw the husband and wife that took us. We had two small beds. I remember crying a lot at first – we used to sob and sob and sob. I was nine and she was seven, and we probably spent an hour crying. After that we'd eat an apple or read something, and go to bed.

BILLETING THE EVACUEES

In each rural area a billeting officer was appointed to find homes for the evacuees. After a long journey the children would line up and wait for a 'host family' to choose them. The person taking the child – the billetor – received a payment from the government of 10 shillings and sixpence. Billeting was compulsory and those who refused to take in evacuees could be taken to court and fined.

LEFT: *A nurse with child evacuees from Plymouth in the garden of the Chaim Weizmann Home at Tapley Park, Instow, North Devon.*

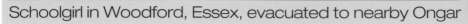
'I DON'T RECALL ANYTHING APART FROM THE BLACKOUT, AND HAVING these black curtains, and the windows with sticky tape in case they got shattered. Some houses had boards that you put up to completely block out the light. I remember a warden shouting, 'Put out that light!' You heard that quite often, because they patrolled the streets. And the food shortages – my sister didn't know what a banana was until after the war, and oranges were kept for pregnant women and small children under five.

We were in the playground and my young sister was crying – lots of little children were crying.

I don't remember my mother saying, 'This is it – you're going.' We were in the playground and my young sister was crying – lots of little children were crying. This was mainly because mothers were left outside the gate, and we were ushered into the school. We all walked to the station with our gas masks round our necks, in a long crocodile from Leytonstone High Road. When we arrived at Ongar Station we walked into the local school hall, where we stood around – and in the centre were the prospective foster mothers, but they walked around as if we were cattle.'

THE BLACKOUT

To make it difficult for enemy bombers to see their targets at night – as even a small amount of light might let a German pilot realise that he was flying above a built-up area – the British government imposed a complete blackout during the war years. Windows had to be hung with thick black curtains or painted with blackout paint and local wardens patrolled the streets checking for signs of light. All street lights were turned off, although later, permission was given for small torches to be used outside.

RIGHT: *Three young ARP Wardens read or write, as they wait for a call out. All are wearing their steel helmets and a row of gas masks can be seen on a shelf in the background.*

Gwendoline Stewart
Schoolgirl evacuated to Ashby-de-la-Zouch

'HELEN STARTED TO CRY WHEN SHE SAW MY MOTHER, AND ASKED, 'Mum, why can't we come home?' My mother asked if she could speak privately to her children, and she was shown into another room. I said, 'Mum, we can't sit down to eat – we have to stand at the table. They don't give us chairs, and we have to eat sardines – and we don't like sardines.' Jack said, 'Look, Mum,' and took down his little trousers and showed his bottom – which was red and raw. Helen said, 'And me!' They had been so hungry that they had broken into the food larder and opened a jar of strawberry jam and taken it to bed with them to eat – and the father had found out and had whipped them. My mother was incensed at the injustice of this – we were just being used for the extra money coming into the house. '

2

FIGHTING THE WAR

LEFT: *A German poster with Nazi flag flying prominently over the land.*

ABOVE: *German navy with flag flying.*

THE GERMAN INVASION

With the German invasion of Denmark and Norway in April 1940 and the sudden sweeping assault of Blitzkrieg – 'lightning war' – across Western Europe on 10 May, the quiet period known as the 'Phoney War' was over.

Wing Commander Kenneth Cross
46 Squadron, RAF

‘WE WERE IN NORWAY FOR ABOUT TWO WEEKS – THEN THE ATTACK ON France started. We listened to the news of the German advance. It was a great disappointment to us when the commander told us that the government had decided to evacuate from north Norway, because we'd captured Narvik and pushed the Germans right back to the Swedish border. In another two weeks the whole of north

LEFT: *Men of the British Expeditionary Force prepare to board trains at Dover after their return from home Dunkirk.*

RIGHT: *April 1940. British troops march into captivity under German guard, following the unsuccessful Allied campaign to turn back the German invasion of Norway.*

Norway would have been ours. But we understood that the amount of shipping required to sustain an expedition at that distance up at Narvik was impossible with the major commitment now being in France. So we were to evacuate.

We were told, "We want you to cover the evacuation of the troops from the various fjords by destroyers, and then, when the evacuation is complete, you can either destroy your aeroplanes or you can fly them up to the extreme north or Norway to Lakselv, where you can dismantle your aeroplanes yourselves, and we will endeavour to get a tramp steamer there. You can load them aboard that way."

I declined that course straight away – as I did the proposal to burn the aeroplanes – as we thought they would be needed at home anyway. I asked if we could make an attempt to land on the *Glorious*.

I did the first landing – and in fact it turned out to be a relatively simple operation. My Hurricane stopped a little over two-thirds up the deck. All seven aircraft came on successfully. We fell into the bunks which were allocated to us. Nobody woke up until mid-afternoon the next day, which was 8th June.

I woke up about half-past three. I went along to the wardroom, and was having a cup of tea when the action stations was sounded. I assumed this was another practice. I went along to my cabin and put on my padded Irvine jacket. For some unknown reason I put the squadron funds, amounting to £200–£300, in an envelope in my inner pocket.

I reported to the bridge, as the CO of the squadron. For the next thirty to forty minutes, the ship was steadily hit. After about an hour or perhaps a little less, the ship began to list very badly, but we were still doing quite a good forward speed, some 12–15 knots. We were zigzagging. I thought she would roll over, she had such a list on. Then eventually the order was given to abandon ship.

We were zigzagging. I thought she would roll over, she had such a list on. Then eventually the order was given to abandon ship.

Carley floats were thrown over the side for the crew and us passengers to swim to when we'd jumped over the side. I asked a naval pilot what was the form on abandoning ship. He said, "When they drop these floats, we're still doing quite a considerable speed, so you want to go pretty quickly afterwards, otherwise you'll have a very long way to swim." So when they dropped a float from the quarter deck, I had my Mae West on and I went over the side, came up like a cork, swam about ten yards and scrambled aboard the Carley float.

Very soon we had twenty or thirty people in the ship. To my great delight Flight Lieutenant Jameson, my number two in the squadron, came swimming along and scrambled aboard the Carley float with me. We sat side by side. Eventually the *Glorious* came to a halt about half a mile away from us. One moment she was there. Then we looked round again and she was gone.

It was rough and very cold. Within a short time some of the sailors began to die. Within three hours the first died. We had between twenty and thirty aboard our float. But within a few hours there were only seven of us left.

> *It was rough and very cold. Within a short time some of the sailors began to die. Within three hours the first died.*

THE FORCE OF THE *BLITZKREIG*

On 10 May the first strike on Western Europe occurred when German paratroops landed in Belgium. The roller coaster of *Blitzkrieg* – the German military strategy of rapid movement into enemy territory with tanks and air support – now swept through Holland and Belgium towards the British Expeditionary Force (BEF) in Northern France. The sheer speed, scale and violence of the invasion took the Allies by surprise and they could offer little resistance as German troops moved towards the Channel coast. The Belgian army surrendered on 28 May. French forces and the BEF fought hard but soon they were in retreat across the Channel.

Father Charles-Roux Jean
Officer with French cavalry

WHEN THE GERMAN ATTACK CAME ON THE 10TH MAY 1940, I WAS IN bed at three in the morning, and there was a frightful noise, and I didn't know what it meant. It sounded like a storm and an earthquake all at the same time. Then I realised that it was an artillery bombardment.

Captain Stewart Carter
Sherwood Foresters (Nottinghamshire & Derbyshire Reg.)

WE HAD DUG IN NEAR THE RIVER LASNE WHEN MY COMPANY COMMANDER sent me to get in touch with the Belgian Army on our left. I found them lined up on the road, not far from our position. I was somewhat surprised to see this, as it rather looked like the end of an exercise in England. So I said to an officer, 'Where are your positions going to be?' as he obviously had none. And he just said they were 'finis'.

LEFT: Near Louvain, Belgium, May 1940, Belgian civilian refugees including one child with a wooden leg – take to the road with few possessions, in hope of finding safety.

ABOVE: *Spring 1940. The Belgian Army, still widely using horse-drawn transport, makes a weary retreat on the Louvain–Brussels road.*

So I said, in my best schoolboy French, 'Well, what do you mean by that And he repeated, 'We are finished.' I thought this was the most extraordinary remark. So I said, 'Do you mean to say you've surrendered?' He said, 'That is it. We have finished the war.' So I was thunderstruck and went back to my major and reported that the Belgian Army had surrendered. The major said, 'Don't be so damn silly. Go back and see them again. I never heard such nonsense.'

So I went back again, knowing full well that they had – and a more senior Belgian officer confirmed this.

The Belgians – well, they were in a very bad way, quite exhausted. But then, of course, we were pretty rough by that time ourselves. But their whole attitude was one of complete dejection, and looking at them more closely, I could see they really had finished.

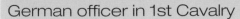

> For the campaign in France we first had to go through Holland. Dutch resistance was courageous and brave, but they were outnumbered, so there was nothing they could do. In France, the French Army was already beaten, and we only had to do the cleaning up. We ended up south of Bordeaux, where relations with the local population were normal. We had a wonderful time. We would have only two hours of duty a day, and then we would go swimming.

THE FALL OF FRANCE

As the Germans advanced, civilians in threatened French towns and villages took to the roads with whatever they could carry, to escape the German occupation. Paris was soon under threat, and on 10 June the French government fled the capital. Paris fell on 14 June and German troops advanced southwards. By 22 June France's surrender was official.

ABOVE: *French civilian refugees. Among them can be seen unarmed French soldiers.*

'THE ROADS WERE ABSOLUTELY jammed solid with civilians of all ages – mostly very young and very old. The old people I shall never forget because it's something I've never seen before – never thought I'd see. Some of them must have been in their eighties, with huge bundles on their backs, bowed right over, walking along these hot roads.

There were mothers pulling prams piled up with belongings, little children hanging on their skirts crying. They weren't walking – they were just trudging along in the heat, virtually worn out. We all responded straight away. All the lads rummaged in their pockets, everywhere. The cookhouse – it was just the field kitchens – started making loads of tea with what water we had, and dishing it out. We felt so sorry for them. I was so fagged out, my legs felt like lead. So all I could do, shells or no shells, was just amble along. I just trudged along, carrying this old Bren gun and all this ammunition stuck in my blouse, in the boiling hot sun. Sweat was pouring off me.

On the 23rd the Germans must have got nearer, because this is where the mortars really took hold of the situation. The mortars came over thick and fast. Nearby there was a Vickers pom-pom on blocks of wood, manned by three gunners. A mortar bomb hit it and the three blokes were just shattered. I ran over to them, and I looked at one poor fellow – his face – his eyes staring up at me. And I thought, 'Well, I can't do anything for him.' I ran back again, and there was this chap, dragging himself on his elbows. He was sobbing, and there were two lines in the sand from his legs – but there was no feet on the end of his legs. I thought. 'God what a terrible thing to happen to anybody!'

The roads were absolutely jammed solid with civilians of all ages – mostly very young and very old.

Weapons of the British Infantry

British infantry soldiers were issued with semi-automatic rifles and light machine guns, the most common of which was called the Bren gun. Its reliabilty made it very popular with soldiers and it became the longest serving weapon in the British Army (August 1938 -– February 2000). Machine guns called Sten guns were also used but were less popular as they tended to jam. Heavy machine guns, such as the Vickers 303, needed a team of men to operate them and were primarily used for defence. Anti-tank weapons (extremely powerful rifles with special armour-piercing bullets) were used, as well as hand grenades, mortars and flamethrowers.

LEFT: *A Bren-gunner, Private W Wheatley of 'A' Company, 6th Battalion, Durham Light Infantry, 50 Division, during the Battle for Normandy.*

Private Denis Hoy
7th Battalion, King's Royal Rifle Corps

‘AT ONE STAGE, WITH MEMBERS OF THE HEADQUARTERS PLATOON, I WAS sent off in a van with rifles and a Bren gun. We were told that three tanks would be coming up the road, and we were to stop them.

It was all quite an Arabian Nights fantasy! I got really past caring about it. I thought, 'I'm going to get killed now, but if I see any Germans I'll shoot them.' I thought, 'This is the end of me – let's just go along with it.' We were soon captured. They made us put our hands over our heads and get into line, and then they went round and searched us to see if we'd got any weapons.

We were marched off until nightfall. Then they just told us to stop, and I just sort of laid down wherever I was. In the morning I found I'd been lying on a pile of sharp stones that they put on roads – and I had no idea. I'd just gone down there, absolutely exhausted, and slept the night through.

On the march, we went into this field, where we were given some watery soup. We got nothing to have it in, so we had it in our tin helmets.

At odd times on this march, the French put out buckets of water for us, and very often the Germans kicked them over as we went by. **'**

Evelyn Jaulmes
Daughter of former British intelligence officer, living in Paris

'We saw the Belgians and the Dutch fleeing with anything they could bring. We knew this was a dangerous period and so we left on the 11th June and two days later the Germans entered Paris. There were thousands and thousands of us with all the cherished things we could bring, mattresses on the tops of cars. Miles and miles of us and we hindered the French army a lot because all the roads were completely blocked by refugees and the army couldn't get their tanks and troops through to the front to fight the Germans. There was such a panic – we all knew the Germans were coming and we had to go. **'**

Left: *Hitler and fellow German officers against the backdrop of the Eiffel Tower in Paris.*

Evacuation at Dunkirk

The last weeks of May 1940 saw the retreating British and French armies assembling on the beaches at Dunkirk, in France. The first priority was to save the men to fight another day and to transport them back to Britain to regroup. It seemed an impossible undertaking but with the massed efforts of the Royal and French Navies, and private vessels of every description, large and small, a total of 338,226 British and French troops were eventually brought back to British shores.

ABOVE: *British troops line up on the beach at Dunkirk to await evacuation.*

Francis Codd
Auxiliary Fire Service in London, aboard the *Massey Shaw*

"GRADUALLY WE COULD SEE DARK SHAPES AGAINST THE SAND – AND THEN we saw that there were hundreds – thousands – of people on this sand, and stretching up to the line of houses which stood, presumably, on the road that ran along the coast. It was an extraordinary sight. Nothing seemed to be happening.

They didn't seem to be moving in any organised way – not marching. They were standing or sitting, but mainly we noticed that they were columns of men stretching down into the sea. We didn't really understand what this was at first – and then it suddenly occurred to us that these were columns of men waiting to be picked up. The first man in the sea was the next man to be picked up.

One of our auxiliaries, Shiner Wright, was a good swimmer, and he went from the *Massey Shaw* some fifty to a hundred yards to a wrecked boat which was right inshore in about two or three feet of water. He swam with what we called the 'grass line', which is a rope that floats on water, and he tied it to the wreck so that we had a fixed line into shallow water. Now there were lots of little rowing boats in the water, mainly sunk or not being used. So they got a rowing boat that would hold very few people, a light rowing boat, and worked it along the line, pulling hand over hand. When we got organised, this worked very well. Whoever was in charge of the column of men lined up near the shore end of the line, detailed six men into the rowing boat to pull along the line 'til they reached the *Massey Shaw*, climb out on board and send their rowing boat back for another half-dozen. In that way I think we took aboard 36 soldiers out of the water that night. **,**

RIGHT: *Tired but safe, men picked up from the beaches of Dunkirk in late May 1940 arrive back in England aboard one of the many ships commandeered to come to their rescue.*

Sergeant Leonard Howard
210 Field Company, Royal Engineers

'It was chaotic. The Germans were very close, and people were being killed. At 21 years old, one hadn't experienced death and people being killed. So it was a bit frightening.

Survival, of course, was the main object in everyone's mind. I saw an RSM walking down the road. He was in his knee breeches and his service dress jacket and cap – and the tears were streaming down his face. He said, 'I never thought that I would see the British Army like this.' And I always remember him. Poor man was absolutely shattered. He was a regular soldier, and the tears were streaming down his face.

We got into Dunkirk around five o'clock in the evening – we hadn't eaten and it was really chaos. The sand was littered with bodies and crowds of chaps all hoping to get off.

I was exhausted, and I went to sleep. I lay in the sand in the dunes, and I slept, because I was really completely exhausted. The next morning, my mate Bill Baldry was still around, and he and I went into the water, hoping to get picked up. But there was no hope. They tried to organise queues, but it was very difficult. People were not only being Stuka-ed, but there was also panic on the beaches themselves.

I saw chaps run into the water screaming...

I saw British men shoot British troops. On one occasion, a small boat came in – and they piled aboard it to such a degree that it was in danger of capsizing. The chap in charge of this boat decided he must take some action. He ordered one man who was hanging on the side to get away – but he didn't, so he shot him through the head. From the people around there was no reaction at all. There was such chaos on the beach that that didn't seem to be out of keeping. There were chaps who were going round the bend. I saw chaps run into the water screaming, because mentally it had got too much for them.'

Bernt Engelman
Luftwaffe pilot

'On the beaches and in the dunes north of Dunkirk, thousands of light and heavy weapons lay in the sands, along with munitions crates, field kitchens, scattered cans of rations and innumerable wrecks of British army trucks.

'Damn!' I exclaimed to Erwin. 'The entire British Army went under here!' Erwin shook his head vigorously. 'On the contrary! A miracle took place here! If the German tanks and Stukas and navy had managed to surround the British here, shooting most of them, and taking the rest prisoner, then England wouldn't have any trained soldiers left. Instead, the British seem to have rescued them all – and a lot of Frenchmen too. Adolf can say goodbye to his Blitzkrieg against England.'

ABOVE: *Dunkirk evacuees – one with a captured German helmet – have a pie and a cup of tea courtesy of a friendly ATS girl as their train fills up at Dover.*

Battle in the Air

By summer 1940, France had been conquered and Hitler's next thought was to invade Britain. As the bulk of his troops and war material would have to be transported by sea, he first needed to gain air superiority over the Channel.

ABOVE: *Supermarine Spitfire taking off from Fowlmere, Cambridgeshire.*
LEFT: *Poster recruiting both men and women to join the war effort.*

THE BATTLE OF BRITAIN

The destruction of the Royal Air Force Fighter Command was essential to Hitler's invasion plan. All possible resources were harnessed into building aircraft and training more fighter pilots to defend the vital radar stations and key airfields on Britain's south coast. The German air force (the Luftwaffe) led by Hermann Goering was a highly dangerous opponent – indeed, Goering had promised that his pilots could destroy the RAF in a month.

Throughout the summer of 1940, Hurricanes and Spitfire fighter planes were in action day in, day out, fighting the Luftwaffe in one of the most crucial battles of the Second World War. Only in late September, was it certain that the tide had been turned and Britain was safe from invasion.

Raymond Cooper
Boy, south of England, aged 14

'I WAS EXCITED WE WERE GOING TO FIGHT THE GERMANS. WE WERE NEAR two squadrons – we used to count them out and count them back in, so we used to know how many were missing. I used to do that every day during the Battle of Britain. I saw so many dogfights during that time – some planes would come quite low and be forced down, and I saw some crash into the hills near my village and saw some fall into the sea. Once I saw some Germans get out of a plane that had crashed into the sea – they had their dinghy out and they thought they were on their way, but they were caught, and that was that.'

Frederick Winterbotham
Secret Intelligence Service

'I THINK THE MOST IMPORTANT SIGNAL WE HAD DECRYPTED THROUGH ULTRA right at the beginning of the Battle of Britain, was Goering establishing his strategy with his commanders. He told them that they were to fly over Britain and bring the whole of the Royal Air Force up to battle, because only in that way could it be destroyed in the time they had.

That was the key for Dowding – to fight the battle with very small units every time they came over – gradually wearing them down and always having aeroplanes to send up. It became evident that Hitler and his generals wouldn't contemplate invasion unless they had absolute control of the air over the Channel.

RIGHT: *Sir Hugh C T Dowding, Commander in Chief of Royal Air Force Fighter Command during the Battle of Britain.*

CODEWORD ULTRA

During the war both sides encrypted their top-secret information. Messages were obscured, usually by being written in code (replacing words with letters, numbers or symbols) or cipher (adding or substituting letters or numbers in a message), so that the enemy could not understand them. Teams of expert codebreakers were employed to try and decrypt – 'unscramble' – enemy information.

The Germans used a unique cipher machine called Enigma and they believed that their messages were impossible to decrypt. However, British codebreakers did eventually break the Enigma cipher and the codeword ULTRA (meaning 'ultra secret') was used to describe the information that they gained from it.

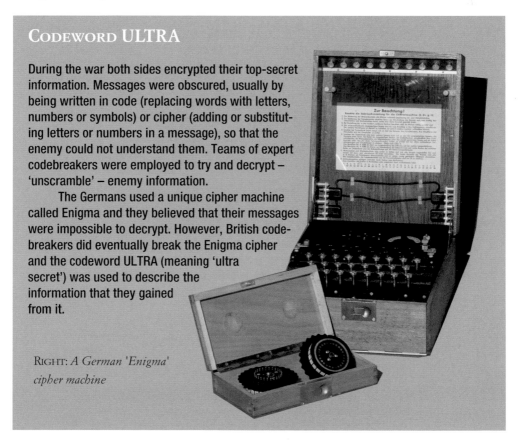

RIGHT: *A German 'Enigma' cipher machine*

Flight Lieutenant Al Deere
54 Squadron, RAF

‘ON THE WAY OUT THERE WAS AN AWFUL gut fear. When you sighted them it really was – it was quite a frightening sight. But once you got into combat there wasn't time to be frightened. But we were frightened – of course we were – the whole bloody time. But if you're in combat, you're so keen to get the other guy and, if you like, save your own skin, that your adrenalin's pumping and there's no room for fright.’

DOGFIGHTS OVER ENGLAND

The term 'dogfight' was used to describe aerial battles that took place between two or more aircraft. During the Battle of Britain most dogfights took place over Southern England, with German Luftwaffe fighter planes such as the Dornier 17, the Heinkel III and the Junkers 87 Stuka, taking on British Hurricanes and Spitfires in fierce and bloody clashes. During the battle the RAF lost 792 planes, the Luftwaffe 1,389.

LEFT: *A Heinkel He III bomber flying over Wapping and the Isle of Dogs in the East End of London.*

'I FLEW AS AN ESCORT TO THE BOMBERS. I HAD SOME OPPORTUNITIES TO shoot the opposition down – but not the luck. For us, it was more important to stop the British planes from shooting at our bombers than to have a dogfight. I came through without being hit. We mostly attacked the River Thames as far as London – targets further away were out of our range. The British flak was very good – they almost didn't have to aim, because our route was so consistent as we were always so worried about running out of fuel. But this changed later on when we could attach extra fuel.'

We mostly attacked the River Thames as far as London – targets further away were out of our range.

RIGHT: *Heinkel He III bombers flying in formation.*

‘WE COULD SEE THE USUAL SWARM OF WHAT LOOKED LIKE LITTLE INSECTS taking shape – it was a large formation of Dornier 217s, escorted by [Messerschmitt ME]109[s]. I was in the leading group of three, then I could see the tracer coming towards me from the whole formation – they had obviously singled me out as a target.

All these things which looked like lethal electric light bulbs kept flashing by, then finally there was a big bang and the aircraft exploded. The scientists reckon the temperature goes up from a cool room temperature at 15,000 feet to 3,000 degrees Centigrade in ten seconds. So, when you consider water boils at 100 degrees, that's quite a temperature change. If you don't get out immediately, you're never going to get out. The beauty of the RAF training came to my rescue and I instinctively reached for the harness and slid the hood back. I rolled the aircraft on to its back, kicked back the control column so the aircraft pointed its nose upwards, but as I was upside down, I popped out like a cork out of a toy gun.

I stupidly wasn't wearing any gloves, so my hands got a terrible burning, and face as well. My mouth and nose were saved by my gas mask. I found myself tumbling head over heels through space. I remember seeing my right arm and extending it, making myself pull the metal ring of the ripcord on my parachute – and that was agony. It was like an electric shock through my burnt hand. Again, you don't have a choice, because, if you don't, the parachute won't open.

I rolled the aircraft on to its back, kicked back the control column so the aircraft pointed its nose upwards, but as I was upside down, I popped out like a cork out of a toy gun.

ABOVE: *This German airman bailed out with his parachute after his plane was shot down by RAF fighters. He is seen holding his parachute and answering a policemen who is taking down details.*

Fortunately, my parachute wasn't on fire. One then took stock of the situation, and I noticed a funny thing had happened. My left shoe and my trousers had been blown off completely by the explosion. I was almost naked from the waist downwards – my legs were slightly burnt. Then I could hear the fight all around me, and it took me about ten minutes to float down into the water.

I had various problems to deal with. First of all, I had to get rid of my parachute, but you had to turn this metal disk on your stomach. You turn it through ninety degrees and then give it a hard thump – but it was difficult because I was badly burnt. Then the parachute was on top of me, so I was really inside a tent with the cords trapping me like an octopus's tentacles. I knew I had to get it away quickly, otherwise I would sink. Again, desperation comes into the issue, so you do turn it, and you do thump it.

The next thing was to blow up my life jacket. I got hold of the rubber tube over my left shoulder, but when I blew into it, all I got was a lot of bubbles.

It had been burnt right through. My face was swelling up at this point, and my eyesight was bad because my swollen eyelids were closing up. The distant view of England, which I could see a few miles away was a bit blurred, but I started vaguely in the right direction.

Then a happy thought came to my mind, and I remembered that in my jacket pocket I had a brandy flask that my dear mother had given me – which I had filled with brandy just as an emergency measure. I thought that this probably qualified as an emergency, so I rolled on my back. This was a painful process, but I got it out and held it between my wrists and undid the screw cap with my teeth. I thought, 'Well, life is going to feel a bit better.' But as I lifted it up to take a swig, a dirty big wave came along and the whole lot went to the bottom of the Channel. I was a bit annoyed about that, but there was nothing else for it, so I continued swimming.

I heard, rather than saw the boat. There were two men in it, and they kept asking me questions. By this time I had been swimming for half an hour, and I was fed up with the whole affair, so when they asked me if I was a Jerry, I'm afraid I let loose with every rude four-letter word that I could think of, and that immediately assured them that I was an RAF officer. They picked me out of the water, and took me to the big ship, where the captain dressed my burns and gave me a cup of tea.

Flight Lieutenant Peter Brothers
32 Squadron, RAF

It was all fairly intense, but the waiting around at base was the hardest part. We'd either sleep, play mahjong or read. When we were 'scrambled', one of our chaps would run to his aircraft, be violently sick, and then jump into his aircraft and be off. Your adrenalin really got going once that bell went. We all swore we'd never have a telephone at home after the war – because as soon as the telephone rang you'd all automatically be at the ready.

THE BLITZ

On 7 September 1940 the Luftwaffe turned its attention to London and, in a massive raid, much of the East End was set on fire. The long-expected assault on British cities had begun.

IF YOU ARE BOMBED OUT
and have no friends to go to

ask a
POLICEMAN
or your **WARDEN**
where to find your
REST CENTRE

ISSUED BY THE MINISTRY OF HEALTH

LEFT: *A poster advising people on what to do if their homes were destroyed by bombs.*

Peter Bennett
Schoolboy in Godalming, Surrey

"I REMEMBER GOING OUT WITH MY DAD. I DON'T KNOW WHERE HE GOT the petrol, but we were taking someone home, and we thought we had seen the sunset. Then we realised that it was the London docks on fire. The sky was red."

Frederick Delve
London-based fireman

"WHEN THEY CAME AT DUSK IT WAS BLACKOUT CONDITIONS, AND fortunately for us, the total area of the London region is 700 square miles, so it wasn't in the same streets every night that the bombs fell. They were obviously

LEFT: *Scene on the Thames with smoke in the background showing the impact of German bombing.*

RIGHT: *Men of the London Auxiliary Fire Service deal with the blazes started by incendiary bombs.*

picking out area by area, which was most helpful to the fire service because we were able, generally, to extinguish most fires before the following night – otherwise they would have formed a beacon for the raiders that were coming later.

I learned after the war that the Germans chose their raid time when the water in the Thames was at its lowest. It was only possible for fire boats to be right in the centre of the river, and for firemen to take hoses ashore it would mean them standing up to their shoulders in mud to struggle ashore with lines of hose.

Ellen Harris
Reuters press reporter at Houses of Parliament

WE GOT A BUS, AND WE'D GONE TWO OR THREE HUNDRED YARDS – as far as Islington Green – and the sirens went. Nobody knew what to do – this was the first ever. We'd had drill and training and what was impressed on everybody was the gas mask. And now, here was the first warning. Your mind immediately flew to the worst of everything. We were all turfed off the buses. Drivers, conductors, everybody, down into a shelter – we stopped right outside Islington Green shelter. As we all went in – mothers carrying little babies with their gas masks on – the wardens were calling out 'Mind the live wires!' They hadn't finished the shelter. That was rather a shock. **'**

SHELTERING FROM THE RAIDS

The sound of the air raid warning let people know that enemy planes were approaching and that it was time to take cover. Large public shelters were built in the cities and almost one and a half million Anderson shelters were distributed to individual homes. These were corrugated-iron structures for use in the garden, but they were not terribly popular, being small, dark and damp. After February 1941, steel Morrison shelters, which had space for two or three people to sleep in, were used inside the house. However, some people preferred to go down to the local underground station, where they would bed down for the night on the crowded platform.

RIGHT: *An Anderson shelter remains intact after a land mine fell a few yards away.*

RIGHT: Men and women sleeping on an Underground platform to keep safe during an air raid.

Elizabeth Quayle
London ARP Unit

"WHEN YOU CAME BACK AT NIGHT ON the underground, of the entire platform, only the bit – the eighteen inches or maybe two foot – near the edge was left, and all the rest were rows of people with their belongings, cats and dogs and children. They were as good-tempered as it was possible to be. Looking back on it, everyone was much more friendly. You would have thought nothing of leaving your bags or your suitcase there – nobody would have taken anything."

THE BOMBING SPREADS

Following the initial raids on London, Liverpool, Belfast, Glasgow, Coventry and other urban areas were attacked during the Blitz, which lasted from September 1940 to May 1941. By the end of 1940, nearly 14,000 civilians had been killed in bombing raids.

THE
BRITISH NAVY
guards the freedom of us all

WAR AT SEA

Throughout the war German U-boat
packs and surface vessels attacked
Allied convoys in the Atlantic,
inflicting heavy losses.
However, the Royal Navy recorded some
significant victories, in particular
the sinking of the Bismarck.

ABOVE: *An aerial view of a convoy. During the war 366,852 tons of*
Allied Merchant shipping were sunk in the Atlantic.
LEFT: *This poster shows the importance of the British Navy.*

Able Seaman Bob Tilburn
Aboard HMS *Hood*, one of only three survivors

'THE *BISMARCK* WAS APPROXIMATELY 300 MILES AWAY. WE SET OFF AFTER her and at 2000 hours, went into action stations because we expected to pick her up at midnight. Then the weather deteriorated and at midnight there was a blizzard, so we couldn't see anything. But we still had reports from the *Suffolk*, saying in which direction they had last seen her. We switched off our radar in case the *Bismarck* could pick up our transmissions and know there was somebody shadowing her. We were travelling at full speed – about 29.5 knots. Then, between 5.00 and 6.00 on the morning of the 24th May, we sighted the *Bismarck* in the distance, turned in towards her and opened fire at about 25,000 yards. I was manning one of the 4-inch AA guns on the port side. The *Bismarck* answered immediately with three shells, each getting closer and closer and closer.

Then the fourth, fifth and sixth shells hit us. Everyone, even the gun crews, was ordered to go into the shelter deck. There were three of us from our gun who didn't take cover. Then a shell hit the upper deck and started a fire. The ammunition in our ready-use locker was on fire and started exploding. The gunner's mate told us to put out the fire, but we said, 'When it stops exploding, we will.' He went back inside to report to the gunnery officer, and at that moment, a shell flew into the shelter and killed the lot – 200 blokes. We three were still alive, lying flat on our faces on the deck with everything going off around us.

He went back inside to report to the gunnery officer, and at that moment, a shell flew into the shelter and killed the lot – 200 blokes.

The next shell came aft, and the ship shook like mad. I was next to the gunshield, so I was protected from the blast, but one of my mates was killed and the other had his side cut open by a splinter. It opened him up like a butcher, and all his innards were coming out. Bits of bodies were falling over the deck, and one hit me on the legs. I thought, 'I'm going to be sick,' so I got up and went to the ship's side to throw up. Then I looked up and saw the bows coming out of the water, and started to strip off – tin hat, gas mask, duffel coat and all the rest. By then the water had reached me and I was swimming.

I had my sea boots on and a very tight belt. I paddled around in the water and took my knife and cut my belt so I could breathe properly. Then I looked around and saw the *Hood* was rolling over on top of me. It wasn't a shadow – it was a big mast coming over on top of me. It caught me across the back of the legs and the radio aerial wrapped around the back of my legs and started pulling me down.

> *I looked up to see the Hood with her bows stuck in the air – then she slid under.*

-I still had my knife in my hands, so I cut my sea-boots off and shot to the surface.

I looked up to see the *Hood* with her bows stuck in the air – then she slid under.

It was 6.00 in the morning. It was dark and cloudy, but there was good visibility. A heavy swell, about fifteen or twenty foot. There wasn't anybody in sight.

Further away I could see a lot of clobber in the water, so I swam over. I thought I would get myself one of those little rafts, made of wood and about a metre square. But they were in a fuel oil slick, and I didn't want to go in. So I paddled around, and I was getting really cold by then. I spotted two other survivors on rafts – Ted Briggs and Midshipman Dundas. But there was nobody else . . . nobody else. No bodies . . . nobody else alive or dead out of 1,400 men. Just we three. '

Otto Peters
German stoker, aboard *Bismarck*

'WHEN WE HEARD THAT THE *HOOD* HAD BEEN SUNK, THERE WAS NO cheering but we did feel pride. Then our captain said that we were being followed by the British Navy. We felt a torpedo strike our rudder – but we didn't know where it had hit. The ship jumped a little bit. I was still in the engine room and I had to stay there for the rest of my shift – but afterwards while carrying out other duties, I went out on deck. It was rainy and windy. The captain came on the radio at about 2000 hours on the 26th May and told us that all the

> *We felt a torpedo strike our rudder – but we didn't know where it had hit.*

Bismarck could now do was sail in a circle and that there was no escape. I was frightened, but as a youngster I didn't quite believe it.

The following morning at about 0700 hours, we were informed that we would have a fight with the British Navy and we were alone, while the British had plenty of cruisers and battleships. A little later, I could hear that we got hit. I had to stay at my battle station and do my duty, but luckily my engine room was not hit. Then the order came from the first officer that we were free and could leave our battle stations. We had to try to get on to deck from the engine room. It was not easy, we had to open all the doors, and when I reached the deck below the main deck, all the lights were out and the water was up to my chest. I felt a hit while we were on this deck. There was another man there and we managed to force the last door open 10 inches. I had to take my leather clothes off to get through the narrow gap.

Finally we arrived on deck. I looked around and the devastation was awful – everything had been shot away and masses and masses of dead comrades lay around. I decided to stay on board as long as the ship stayed afloat so that I could keep my strength. It was windy and stormy. The ship was half submerged. A huge wave washed over the ship but I managed to grip something and I wasn't knocked overboard until a second wave threw me into the water. I was wearing a life jacket and I was a good swimmer and

RIGHT: *Men of the sinking German battleship* Bismarck *are hauled to safety aboard HMS* Dorsetshire, *27 May 1941. Of a crew of 2,200, just 115 were rescued.*

I tried to swim away. The sea was very cold but I was so excited that I didn't feel it. I was thinking about my girlfriend in Hamburg and how I had to stay alive to see her again. There was no wood or wreckage around me to cling to – which was lucky because in areas where there was a lot of wood and wreckage, there was also a lot of oil. There were shipmates nearby and we called to each other that whichever of us survived should tell the other's parents what happened. I was near one guy I knew well who wasn't saved, and afterwards I wrote a letter to his parents.

After a couple of minutes, I turned around and I saw the ship turning upside down and going right down. About fifteen minutes later, I saw a ship ahead of me through a rainy wall and I swam towards it. The ship was the *Dorsetshire* but I didn't know it at the time.

There were shipmates nearby and we called to each other that whichever of us survived should tell the other's parents what happened.

Petty Officer Joseph Willetts
Aboard HMS *Prince of Wales*

WE WERE PERFECTLY STILL, ALL OF US, BECAUSE WE KNEW THERE WAS some imminent news. He said, 'This is the captain. I have just received a message from Admiralty, which I must read to you. The *Bismarck* is sunk.' That was the message – and there was an immediate cheer all over the ship. As things went quiet, the captain said, 'Gentlemen, I'm sure that you will agree that this is the end of a very gallant ship.'

ACTION IN THE DESERT

For three years, Axis and Allied forces pursued each other over the hostile terrain of the North African desert. The tide finally turned in the Allies' favour at the Second Battle of El Alamein in 1942.

ABOVE: *A soldier fighting in the desert. The conditions, including extreme temperatures of hot and cold made life uncomfortable.*

THE WESTERN DESERT, 1940–41

In September 1940 Italian forces invaded Egypt, but were defeated by the British army in early 1941. Following their ally's collapse, German forces – the Afrika Korps under the command of General Rommel – were sent to the Western Desert and set about reclaiming the territory the Italians had lost. In June, British troops went into action to relieve the base at Tobruk, which had been surrounded since April, but were driven back, sustaining over a thousand casualties and losing more than a hundred tanks.

Sergeant Stephen Dawson
339 Battery, 104th Regiment, Royal Artillery

WE KNEW SOMETHING WAS GOING ON WHEN WE WERE ORDERED TO travel up to Tobruk in about January 1941, because of the tension in the air – but we were just ordinary soldiers at that time, and nobody told us anything. On the way there, the convoy came to a brief halt. We'd found the body of a young British officer. He'd been shot across the chest. He had blue eyes and fair hair, with a

*We started to dig a grave and I made
a little plywood cross – but suddenly
we were told to go again, and we had to leave
him there – somebody's son.*

revolver in his hand – just this one solitary object lying in the middle of the vast desert. We started to dig a grave and I made a little plywood cross – but suddenly we were told to go again, and we had to leave him there – somebody's son. **,**

LEFT: *Transport Column of the Afrika Korps in the Desert Campaign of 1941–42.*

RIGHT: *Australian troops stand in fox-holes, dug in on the front line at Tobruk, where the garrison was the focus of continual fighting as the stronghold changed hands several times during the course of the year.*

‘I DIVED INTO THE SLIT TRENCH AND ANOTHER YOUNG CHAPPIE DIVED ON top of me. When the bombs had finished exploding and the aircraft were going away I said, 'Come on, get up, Phil!' He didn't move and I got up and he sort of flopped over on his back. I said, 'What's the matter are you hit?' I couldn't see a mark on him, but he was obviously out – in fact, he was dead. A small piece of shrapnel as big as would cover a thumb nail had gone into the back of his neck and must have severed the spinal column and killed him, just like that.

There was one very big chap with us, and when a dive-bombing raid came, he dived into the Boyes anti-tank rifle pit. He and the 500-pounder had a race for it – and the 500-pound bomb won. He was not mutilated as such – I think it was the blast that killed him – because when we picked him up it was rather like picking up a fish – he was all floppy. It must have broken every bone in his body.’

‘WE MOVED UP TO TOBRUK IN APRIL 1941. IT WAS A VERY FLAT PLACE – not a sandy desert like the Sahara – a scrubby sort of desert, and there was an incredible shortage of water. We used to get desperately thirsty. We were living in these cement dugouts with slit trenches, and doing night patrols. Night after night we set out on patrols, and we'd go so far, then we'd go to ground. Then we just lay there, a listening patrol, lying there for hours. It would get bitterly, bitterly cold, and you just hoped that you surprised the Germans and they didn't surprise you.’

Fighting in the Desert

The desert was a bleak and unknown environment for the European soldiers. The extreme temperatures – hot by day and cold by night – made life very uncomfortable. Visibility was hampered by sandstorms and dust and navigation was difficult in a landscape with few landmarks. Thirst was a constant problem as water supplies were scarce.
The soldiers were also plagued by flies, which carried sand fly fever and caused desert sores – a type of ulcer made by the flies' maggots eating the flesh.

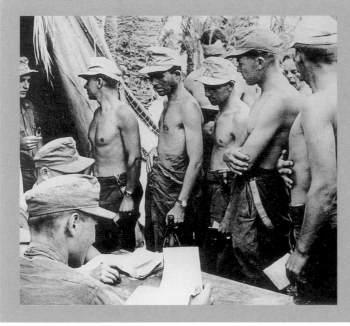

LEFT: *German troops being vaccinated at an oasis in the Western Desert.*

Squadron Leader Fred Rosier
229 Squadron, RAF

6 LIFE IN THE WESTERN DESERT WAS TOUGH AND DEMANDING. WE HAD TO put up with the extremes of heat and cold – the sandstorms which got worse and, even more depressing as time went on, the flies (particularly where the Italians had been), the shortage of water, the monotony of the daily diet of bully beef and hard biscuits – and the fear . . . that feeling in the pit of the stomach before going on operations. 9

The Second Battle of El Alamein

By early 1942 the Germans had the upper hand, but the tide began to turn when Montgomery took command of the British Eighth Army on 18 August, following an inconclusive battle at El Alamein on 2 July. The British now inflicted heavy losses on Rommel's troops and, with the greatest artillery barrage ever delivered, the Second Battle of El Alamein began on 23 October. Rommel's troops were soon in retreat and on 13 November the Allies retook Tobruk.

Sergeant John Longstaff
2nd Battalion, Rifle Brigade

❝Before Montgomery, we never knew what our role was – where we were going, what was going to happen, who was on our left flank, right flank – who were our reserves. We didn't even know who the enemy was prior to Montgomery. He gave the order that every soldier will be told who is on his left and who is on his right – who is behind him and who is in front of him, and he will be told what he's going to do. When a man is told those things, he starts getting confidence. He doesn't feel that he's fighting by himself.❞

Martin Ranft
German gunner, 220th Artillery Regiment, Afrika Korps

❝El Alamein was my home for quite a while, because we were stopped. On the 23rd October, nine o'clock in the evening, that's when we heard that terrible artillery fire from the British line. I was facing the front line and suddenly the whole sky was red with the gunfire. The shells were howling over you and exploding all around you – it was just horrible. We thought then that the world was coming to an end.❞

Corporal Peter Taylor
2nd Battalion, Rifle Brigade

‘IT WAS ABOUT THE 12TH DAY OF ALAMEIN WHEN THE ENEMY REALLY started to go. The desert was littered with Alpine boots and rucksacks with a cover which was made with the hide of a deer or elk or something – hair-covered rucksacks. We found out afterwards that this Alpine regiment had been hurriedly sent from Italy across to Tripoli and whistled down to the battlefield almost before they could pause for breath. All their Alpine boots had been hung on the outside of their packs. They'd been put straight into the front line to hold positions. This stuff was all over the place – the dross of an army, if you like – tins and cans and bullets and guns and rifles, boots, packs, hats – a hundred and one things everywhere. Burnt-out vehicles and tanks – and a few graves, though not many. The dead on our side had all been taken away. They were taken away and buried. I should imagine the engineers had burial details – had graves prepared ready for the possible number of casualties. The casualty evacuation and withdrawal of people of ours who were killed was incredible. The wounded were got away extremely quickly in jeeps and little armoured cars with stretchers built on to the back of them – strap him down and whoosh – off. They'd have an orderly sitting on the back to see the chap didn't get bounced out. The medical evacuation was heartening because people had been told, 'If you get wounded, you'll be whipped away straight away.' We'd never had this sort of thing before.

Everything had been thought of – that was why the spirit was so good. After years of being pushed about by the Axis forces, at last we were holding our own and doing a bit better than holding our own. We were actually beating them.’

ABOVE: *El Alamein, the Western Desert, 1942. With visibility obscured British infantry advance.*

WAR IN THE MEDITERRANEAN

Two strategically important islands,
Crete and Malta, found themselves at
the centre of a raging battle
between Allied and Axis powers
for naval control of the Mediterranean.

ABOVE: *A street in Malta after bombing reduced it to rubble.*

Sergeant Frederick Birch
No. 7 Commando

'THE MESSAGE CAME THAT THE WITHDRAWAL HAD STARTED – ALL NON-combatant troops were to get away from the area completely. We would be fighting a rearguard action with some Australians and New Zealanders – the principle being that we would hold a line for the day to let the others get away.

As soon as it became dark, we used to send out front patrols and create a bit of a disturbance – then draw back. Then the whole line would draw back and go through a line that had been formed by the other troops who were behind us. We would withdraw through them and form another line a matter of two or three miles behind them, across the road and into the hills.

We'd have a sleep during the day, then at night this other line would then withdraw through us as soon as it became dark. We would have to hold that line while they did the same sort of thing.

The very last line that we formed, we'd almost come to the end of the queue. All troops were channelled into this very narrow road, which ran down through a fishing village in a bay. There wasn't very much room on the road, and we were still a mile and a half from the beach. We were lined up there and wondering what we should do then, because we were forming a line and during the night the other troops that had formed the line ahead of us would be passing through us – but they would have nowhere to go. So we were wondering what we were going do when it started to become dusk.

Then the word came up like a rustle to start with, and as it came nearer, we could make out that there were no more boats and that we were at the point of surrender here on the island. A few people got a bit hysterical – I remember some of the lads crying out, 'We can't surrender. British troops don't do this sort of thing.' I had my section with me, and I said, 'We're not staying here on this road. Come on, get away from this lot,' because that sort of hysteria, I felt, was catching.

When we got to the edge of the cliff we found a hole in the ground, and there was a fellow there. He said, 'There's a cave here, lads. Come on in.' So we went down through the hole into the cave – a great big water-level cave, which the tide came right into at the bottom. We thought we might be safe there for a while.

A few people got a bit hysterical – I remember some of the lads crying out, 'We can't surrender. British troops don't do this sort of thing.'

LEFT: *German planes attacking the Greek island of Crete.*

We kept watch all day, and we saw a few Germans move into the village, and we heard the sound of the Germans chivvying our chaps together in various places – then above the sounds during the day, we heard a British Tommy calling out for tombola. They were playing tombola under these circumstances!

The following day we found a landing craft, fixed the engine and got away to another island occupied by the British. '

Lieutenant-Commander Roger Hill
Aboard Hunt-class destroyer HMS *Ledbury*

'OPERATION PEDESTAL WAS THE LAST ALL-OUT ATTEMPT TO GET A CONVOY of merchant ships through to Malta. Their food was running out and they had no aviation fuel, no submarine diesel and nothing for the dockyard. Malta had virtually come to a halt.

If the convoy failed, Malta would have to surrender. The Governor of Malta, Lord Gort, said to me, 'You can make the garrison eat their belts, but the 300,000 civilians have to be fed or evacuated.'

If the convoy failed, Malta would have to surrender.

The convoy of over 50 ships left Gibraltar on the 9th August 1942. Thirteen merchant ships and the 10,000-ton Texaco tanker *Ohio* steamed in four columns. They were all big, fast ships, and the speed of the convoy was 15 knots. Around them was a screen of 26 destroyers. Close round the convoy were the anti-aircraft destroyers, like my *Ledbury*, and the battleships *Nelson* and *Rodney* – each of which had nine 16-inch guns – steamed astern of the two outside columns. The anti-aircraft ship *Cairo* had a roving commission near the convoy and *Jaunty*, an ocean tug, followed along behind.

Three aircraft carriers, *Victorious*, *Indomitable* and *Eagle*, followed the convoy inside the destroyer screen. They carried a total of 72 fighters and were constantly altering course into the wind to fly off and land on the patrols. The cruisers *Sirius*, *Phoebe* and *Charybdis* careered about, keeping an anti-aircraft guard on the carriers. There was also an old aircraft-carrier, *Furious*, with her own destroyer screen, whose job it was to fly off 38 Spitfires when we were about 500 miles from Malta, as reinforcements for Malta's depleted squadrons.

As we approached down the Mediterranean, we were entering a cauldron of attack. Crete and Greece were in German hands, and would be used for air attack – then the long toe of Italy, Sardinia and Sicily was all aerodromes. About 20 submarines and 40 E-boats were also waiting for us. It was just like another Charge of the Light Brigade.'

It was just like another Charge of the Light Brigade.

Squadron Leader 'Laddie' Lucas
249 Squadron, RAF

'THE LAST VITAL ELEMENT THAT SHOULD BE MENTIONED ABOUT MALTA is that the island obviously depended, for its supplies, on what the convoys could bring in. And because everyone was always hungry, this spectre of starvation was always there. In my time, from February to the end of July 1942, the Navy tried

ABOVE: *'Laddie' Lucas. During the siege of Malta, he commanded 249 Squadron, based at Takali.*

to run through four seaborne convoys. The February convoy from Alexandria had to turn back as it was going through Bomb Alley, between Crete and the Libyan coast – the narrows there were the most terrible place. The Germans were bombing it from Crete and Libya. In March, the convoy with *Breconshire*, *Pampas* and *Talabot* came from Alexandria. As it approached Malta, there was very low cloud – a mistral really – with wind and rain, and it was absolutely made for the Germans to go darting in and out as they attacked the ships. *Pampas* and *Talabot* made Grand Harbour, but as soon as they were in, they got bombed, and that was that. *Breconshire* had to be towed in and beached. Then she was bombed. They got a certain amount of stuff off the ships – probably about 5,000 or 6,000 tons – before they were sunk, but not much more. So that was the March convoy.

We were getting pretty low. Food really was beginning to get short, morale was beginning to fall, and the civilians were having their belts pulled in by the fortnight. The next attempt was in June. There were two convoys. They had this idea that if they ran two convoys together, one from Gibraltar and the other from Alexandria, it would divide the Germans' and the Italians' attacking strength. The one from the east, from Alexandria, when it was going through Bomb Alley, spotted the Italian fleet coming down from the north-east, so they were forced to turn round and go back. That was awful. The one from Gibraltar had started out with six merchant ships and in the end only two got into Grand Harbour. It was the most terrible fight. We could see a third, the US oiler *Kentucky*, which we so badly wanted, sunk as it approached the final run-in. Of the two which reached Grand Harbour, quite a lot of stuff was unloaded – enough to keep us going until August, when the 'Santa Maria' or 'Pedestal' convoy fought its way through.

After a couple of minutes, I turned around and I saw the ship turning upside down and going right down. About fifteen minutes later, I saw a ship ahead of me through a rainy wall and I swam towards it. The ship was the *Dorsetshire* but I didn't know it at the time. **'**

Lieutenant-Commander Roger Hill
Aboard Hunt-class destroyer HMS *Ledbury*

'In the early morning, as we approached Malta, I walked round the ship and looked at the sleeping members of my crew. They were lying in duffle coats, one head on another chap's tummy, faces all sunburnt and lined

RIGHT: *A building in Malta takes a direct hit from a German bomb.*

with the strain of the last few days. I felt proud of them, and grateful we had got through it all without a single casualty. The pom-pom's crew were closed up and ready, training their guns. I climbed up and said, 'Good morning, aren't you going to get any sleep?' and they said, 'Oh no, please sir, just one more attack, can't we have one more attack?' I said, 'Christ almighty, haven't you had enough attacks?' They were great people.

At daylight we came round the corner to the entrance to the Grand Harbour. I pushed the *Ohio* round with my bows and followed her in. It was the most wonderful moment of my life. The battlements of Malta were black with thousands of people, all cheering and shouting and there were bands playing everywhere. It was the most amazing sight to see all these people who had suffered so much, cheering us.

The *Ohio* was pushed by tugs to the wharf to discharge her oil. Her stern was so low now that water was washing over her after deck. Within five minutes they were pumping her out in case she was sunk by enemy bombing.

We berthed the *Ledbury* in the French creek. I went quickly around the ship, looked in on the wounded, then got some dope from Doc, took off my clothes and then, oh boy, did I sleep. **,**

THE ITALIAN CAMPAIGN

In 1943 Allied forces launched an invasion of Italy, landing on Sicily in July, followed by an assault on the mainland at Salerno in September. The Allied advance met with heavy German opposition.

ABOVE: *German troops in action building defences on the Mediterranean Coast.*

'It was cold. You could find yourself a coat or the odd thing, but for a few weeks it was grim. We didn't wait for stuff to come through to us – we just got on with it.

After the Sangro we joined up with the 2nd New Zealand Division – we had been everybody's poor relations until then. We went on to Lanciano, a little up the coast. By December 1943 the 1st Airborne Division had gone home. We stayed on as the 2nd Independent Brigade Group – it was a fairly big unit, spanning the three infantry battalions, the 4th, 5th (Scottish) and 6th (Royal Welch), with a squadron of engineers, a battery of gunners and even a glider-pilot section.

Just before Christmas we had taken a place called Casoli, a village on top of a hill, seemingly a favourite place for villages in that part of Italy. We set up our position on a day when it was snowing. We dug our mortar pits four or five feet down, did one or two shoots during the day, and then at night the snow really came down. We were just below a ridge about ten feet high. I went into my slit trench, put my groundsheet on top of me and in next to no time I was asleep, sitting on my steel helmet to keep out of the wet trench. I was found absolutely snowed under and had to be dug out. If they hadn't found me I would still have been there now, frozen solid. My sergeant gave me a tot of rum to thaw me out.

Throughout this time our casualties were coming from shell and mortar fire. At Arielle, in front of Chieti, the route

> *I was found absolutely snowed under and had to be dug out. If they hadn't found me I would still have been there now, frozen solid.*

LEFT: *A landing craft at Salerno lays down its own smoke screen to provide cover for the arrival of British troops.*

We used to go down it like a bat out of hell – yet every day a supply truck would get blown up.

coming up to our position from rear echelon was under such constant shell fire that it became known as the 'mad mile'. You were more likely to get killed going back to base there than staying in the line. We used to go down it like a bat out of hell – yet every day a supply truck would get blown up.

Every time the Germans stopped they got into a prepared position which they defended. Our brigade never ever went back – always forward – but the Germans had mountains, rivers or prepared defences to pull back to. While they were holding one defensive line, they were getting another ready. We were constantly having to find our way in – they could call the tune. ,

'THE TERRAIN WAS HARD AND THE ALLIED FIGHTER-BOMBERS WERE very effective . You couldn't walk on the road. Even if you were on a bicycle, they would come down and shoot at you. The firepower of the Allied forces was enormous. Even to this day, I can't understand why they didn't achieve more at that time. They were far superior to the German forces. We were positioned forward on the bend of the river and during the night, the Allies bombed and strafed the roads. We needed it to defend ourselves, but we needed every bullet. We still had a very good fighting force. **'**

We still had a very good fighting force.

RIGHT: *A German 40mm Anti-Aircraft gun emplaced in Sicily.*

The Liberation of Rome 1944

The Germans had reinforced the area around the monastery of Monte Cassino and months of bitter fighting with heavy casualties ensued. Four major battles were fought before Cassino fell to the Allies, the road to Rome was opened, and the city was liberated on 4 June – two days before D-Day in Normandy.

ABOVE: *Polish troops hurl grenades during the tough fighting at the battle of Monte Cassino.*

Captain Anthony Harvey
1/5th Battalion, Royal Gurkha Rifles

'WE TURNED DUE EAST FROM FLORENCE AND HAD GONE UP THROUGH a little village called Marudi. We had to go over the spine of the country – which wasn't terribly high. It was a lovely sunny day, and I had gone forward with the patrol.

The leading scout, Thaman, came upon two Germans in a sentry post. Luckily for him, they were both asleep. He charged with his kukri and they both surrendered. The German position somehow was alerted to the fact that their sentries had been captured. Within a very short time, mortar fire of some intensity was coming down on our position.

We couldn't move forward, and a message came from the leading section commander that we were to retire. There was a sudden lull in the firing and I, with my runner, ran for it. What we didn't know until afterwards was that Rifleman Thaman had gone to the top of the hill and had seen the rear positions of the Germans and engaged them with grenades. He had then fired his Tommy gun until his ammunition ran out. He then grabbed a Bren gun from one of his chums and said to them, 'Run for it. I'll keep the Germans' heads down.' He continued firing, in an exposed position, until he was shot through the throat. He died, but the rest of us got away. There is no doubt that he saved our lives, and long after this courageous action, a court of inquiry was set up and all the witnesses were called and told what they knew about his enormous bravery. As a result, he was awarded the Victoria Cross.

THE VICTORIA CROSS (VC)

Being awarded the Victoria Cross is the highest recognition a British soldier, sailor or airman can receive for 'most conspicuous bravery, a daring or pre-eminent act of valour, self-sacrifice or extreme devotion to duty in the presence of the enemy'. The Victoria Cross can be awarded to members of the British or Commonwealth Armed Forces and civilians under military command. The George Cross is the civilian equivalent of the Victoria Cross.

RIGHT: *The Victoria Cross medal.*

RIGHT: *In the battle for Cassino, Italy, May 1944, British crews manning 4.2-inch mortars brace themselves against the deafening noise of their own bombardment.*

Sergeant Gus Platts
6th Parachute Battalion

'ABOUT ELEVEN O'CLOCK AT NIGHT THE BALLOON WENT UP. SOMETHING like 1,600 guns went off at the same moment. That's forgetting all the mortars – we were just small fry, firing on targets already selected. It was like the earth opening – a tremendous noise – and the whole mountain lit up. And we had a hell of a shoot ourselves. We ranged on a target – a crossroads or an area where there were German positions – and fired continuously until the barrels were red-hot. We had to urinate on them to get them cool. All night we were firing. We pulled out at dawn the following morning, when the attack had gone through, and the Germans were moving back to their next defensive line. Cassino had been broken at last!'

It was like the earth opening – a tremendous noise – and the whole mountain lit up.

THE FAR EAST

The Japanese attack on the US fleet at Pearl Harbor in December 1941 had brought the Americans into the war, now a truly global conflict. Japan continued her assault and by June 1942 had taken the British colonies of Hong Kong, Malaya and Singapore.

ABOVE: *In the heart of the jungle a British mortar team works in the heat and ear-shatterng din of battle.*

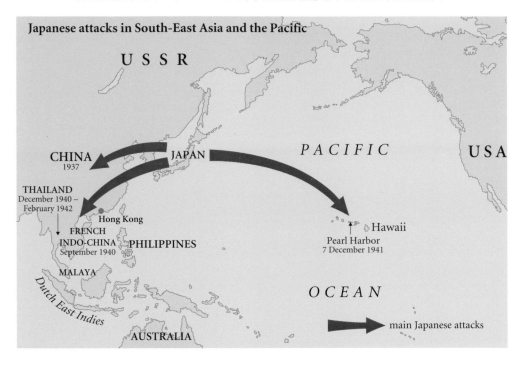

ABOVE: *A map showing the scale and targets of Japanese attacks in the Far East.*

Petty Officer John Gaynor
Aboard HMS *Prince of Wales*

'GIVE THE JAPANESE TORPEDO PILOTS THEIR DUE, THEY PRESSED HOME their attacks. The *Repulse* was gone – she turned upside down, and down she went. By now we had begun to take a list to the port – which meant that the starboard side was coming up out of the water. All battleships, to protect their vitals, have a nice, thick, perhaps eight- or twelve-inch armoured belt stretched along where a shell is liable to strike. But if you lift the ship up, the armour belt finishes and you expose the underbelly. The Japanese pilots knew that, so in

On 10 December 1941, Japanese bombers attacked and sank HMS *Prince of Wales* and HMS *Repulse* off the coast of Malaya. The loss of these two great ships left troops on the mainland vulnerable and there was furious activity to strengthen defences as news of the Japanese advance through Malaya reached Singapore. Hong Kong had surrendered to the Japanese on Christmas Day and Singapore fell on 15 February 1942. Thousands of Allied servicemen were rounded up and taken prisoner.

Then the order came from the bridge to abandon ship – and I thought, 'Oh, I've never done this before.'

came the torpedoes – and crunched into the ship. And now she begins to settle back again. One minute she was looking like she was going over to port – then she rocked back to starboard. Then the order came from the bridge to abandon ship – and I thought, 'Oh, I've never done this before.'

As the ship gradually turned, I hung on to a ventilator, which would be about two-thirds of the way up – uphill, in other words. Then from there, as the ship gradually turned turtle, I managed to get up on the top of the ship. I'm forever climbing upwards now. The ship is turning, and I'm climbing upwards – then I walk down the ship's side – which is now horizontal, and then find myself going over a lovely curve. Now I'm on the bottom of the ship, still floating. So I sit between the two great twin keels of the ship and I look towards the stern, where I see four enormous propellers, still idly turning, though the ship is upside down. As I looked down, I see from underneath the stern that the water now is gradually coming up towards me. What I didn't realise at the time is that the ship is going down – that's why the water is coming towards me. But it's a queer sensation, to stand on something solid, to look at the water and then the water's coming towards you, like the tide coming in.

ABOVE: *As the stricken HMS* Prince of Wales *lists dangerously following the Japanese air attack, her crew scramble for safety.*

I floated on a chunk of wood until I was picked up. A lot of the people that were brought on board, with oil fuel and shock had died. They were stacking the bodies like you would firewood in rows of five – five one way, five another. I always remember gazing into the eyes of a fellow who was a messmate of mine. He was dead, but he didn't seem to have a mark on him. I felt like saying, 'What are you doing there?'

They were stacking the bodies like you would firewood in rows of five – five one way, five another.

'BEFORE I WAS CAPTURED I REMEMBER THE DEAD AND DYING MEN WE were forced to leave behind as the Japanese forced us to retreat up the Malay Peninsula. I remember the hundreds of dead I saw on the streets of Singapore. We were marched to Changi and then moved to a barracks in Singapore town and ordered to sign a paper saying we would not escape. We all refused. But the conditions were like the Black Hole of Calcutta and our senior officers agreed to sign under protest because they were worried about an epidemic.

I was then transported to Thailand to the base camp at Ban Pong. The latrines there were full of great big maggots. I'd had enough. Because the Japs thought no

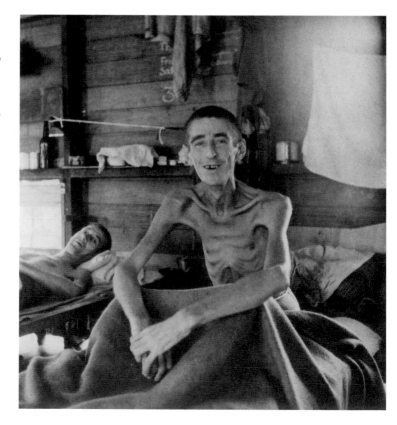

RIGHT: *Jack Sharpe survived illness, starvation and solitary confinement to defy his Japanese captors. Despite weighing only four stone he still managed to take the few faltering steps to leave Outram Road Jail.*

ABOVE: *As the Japanese advance reached the British base of Singapore, on 15 February 1942, running out of water and with little ammunition left, General Percival had no alternative but to surrender.*

They cocked their rifles. I knew for certain I was going to die.

one would escape the guards were thin on the ground. I got out of the camp and headed north but after two days I was captured by a local Thai who had a large gun like a blunderbuss.

I was handed over to a Japanese lieutenant who lined me up in front of a firing squad. They cocked their rifles. I knew for certain I was going to die. Then all of a sudden a Japanese colonel arrived and struck the lieutenant in charge. They were jabbering in Japanese and I was wondering whether they were going to shoot me or not.

In the end the colonel came across and beat the living daylights out of me with his scabbard. Every time I fell he booted me and told me to get up. My hands were then tightly strapped and I was marched back to Ban Pong and handed over to a guard. '

War in Burma

The British colony of Burma was strategically important as a stepping stone into India. In late 1941 the advancing Japanese attacked Burma, and the capital, Rangoon, fell in March 1942. British troops were forced to make a hurried withdrawal.

After the failure of the Japanese 'invasion' of India, the Allies were ready to drive back the Japanese and win back Burma by late 1944. The Japanese proved an unpredictable and ruthless enemy, willing to sacrifice themselves rather than be captured. British losses were heavy.

ABOVE: *The Chinese 22 Division fighting in the Burmese jungle.*

Second Lieutenant John Randle
7/10th Baluch Regiment

‘During the night the Japanese attacked and wiped out my platoon, and a platoon of A Company. As I was moving to Myainggale with my remaining two platoons, I ran into the middle of a Japanese regiment just getting across and taking up positions on the west bank of the Salween. I had a hairy old night, lost a few chaps, but managed to get my two platoons out and back to the main position.

The Japs cut in behind us and we could hear the runner screaming as they killed him with swords and bayonets.

We were in single file when a man charged into our column. I thought it was one of my soldiers running away, and shouted at him. It was a Jap who ran off into the bush. A couple of Japs were then shot by my men, the first dead Jap I had seen. There was quite a lot of firing, and I realised there were quite a lot of Japs about. I tried to get through on my radio, which didn't work. So I sent my runner, the company bugler, back with a message to my CO. The Japs cut in behind us and we could hear the runner screaming as they killed him with swords and bayonets. This was followed by an enormous lot of firing a couple of miles away from the base we were going to relieve. The Japs were running about, in a fair state of confusion too, having just come across the river. We had no idea what tactics we should adopt. I just formed a circle, which looking back was the best thing to do: river on one side, Japs on two sides. It was pure luck not cleverness. It was clear to me there were a considerable number of Japs to the south of me, so I decided to return to the battalion position.

The next day they dive-bombed our positions near the airfield at Chiang Mai across the Thai border. That night the CO decided to send out one of my platoons on patrol. God knows what for. So I was down to one platoon, and a section of MMGs. At about twelve o'clock the Japs came in and we had hand-to-hand fighting. They overran us and C Company. They came in with no artillery support in what started as a silent night attack. When they got close, they screamed banzai and came charging in, shoulder-to-shoulder. The Vickers fired across my front and caused heavy casualties to the Japs, but they surged into Company HQ, where I killed the chap coming for me, while my CSM was grappling with another, but my batman was killed by a grenade. Just before dawn, realising if we stayed we would get taken prisoner, we charged out and then lay up about 150 yards away, and after first light heard a second assault going in, on Battalion HQ. We then had a pause, but at seven o'clock the next morning they finished us off. We lost 289 killed, and had 229 taken prisoner in our first engagement. It took me two days to get back to our lines. We were staked out there like a goat for the Jap tiger and sacrificed for no reason. The CO was killed and we lost over 60 per cent of our officers. Only about fifty of the Battalion got away. With the exception of one officer, the Japs butchered all our wounded. News of this got back to us and this conditioned mine and the whole Battalion's attitude towards the Japs. We were not merciful to them for the rest of the war. We didn't take any prisoners.

The Japs fought with great ferocity and courage.

The Japs fought with great ferocity and courage. We were arrogant about the Japs: we regarded them as coolies. We thought of them as third-rate. My goodness me, we soon changed our tune. We had no idea about jungle fighting, no pamphlets, doctrine etc. Not only were we raw troops, we were doing something entirely new.

JUNGLE WARFARE

The jungle proved deadly in many ways other than fighting. Allied soldiers were unused to this kind of environment and the heat and humidity affected them greatly. Deadly tropical diseases such as malaria, dysentery and typhus were rife and water supplies were scarce. Men would carry heavy equipment through thick jungle in temperatures as high as 40°C. Many suffered from trench foot and septic cuts because of the damp conditions.

RIGHT: *An RAF wireless unit in North Burma arranges for food and supplies to be dropped.*

ABOVE: *British soldiers search through long grass for Japanese snipers while covered by a Bren gun team.*

Captain Alexander Wilson
2nd British Infantry Division's jungle battle school

'MOST BRITISH PEOPLE, MANY BROUGHT UP IN TOWNS, HAVE NEVER really been in the dark, because there are always street lamps, or some sort of light. Few of our soldiers had ever been alone at night. We have lost our sense of hearing and smell. These are basic animal-like instincts which are vital in the jungle. The Japs smelt different to us, and you could smell them in a defensive position, or if they had recently passed down a track. The Japs smelt rather like scented powder. Indians smelt differently to us too – it depends on what you eat.

At night you feel very much on your own and are susceptible to noises deliberately made by the enemy, and you shoot at these, and at shadows, which you mustn't do. Slim's adage was, 'the answer to noise is silence'. It was almost a crime to shoot without having a corpse to show for it in the morning. The antidote is endless training at night. '

Pilot Officer Basil Hewes
82 Squadron, RAF

'ONCE A WATER BUFFALO STROLLED ACROSS A FORWARD STRIP AT KALEWA as a Mosquito was taking off. The pilot didn't see it, the aircraft caught fire, and as we had no fire or crash equipment we had to watch them burn to death. The operating conditions were more dangerous than the Japs. If you landed in the jungle, the chances of getting out were remote. **'**

ASSAULT ON EAST INDIA

In March 1944 the Japanese launched a full-scale assault on eastern India, but by this stage, British and Indian forces had gained in strength and experience. The British Fourteenth Army fought the Japanese to a standstill at the Indian towns of Kohima and Imphal. If they had fallen, then India could have been invaded.

Major John Winstanley
4th Battalion, Royal West Kent Regiment

'THE 4TH ROYAL WEST KENTS, THE ASSAM RIFLES AND ODDS AND SODS defended Kohima against an entire Jap Division in a 14-day siege. The perimeter shrank and shrank until it only included the Tennis Court and Garrison Hill where the final stand took place. At first B Company were only observers on Kuki Picket. After five days we were ordered to relieve A Company on the Tennis Court. On the other side the ground fell away – that's where the Japs were, only fifty yards away. The battle took place on the Tennis Court – we shot them and grenaded them on the Tennis Court. We held that Tennis Court against desperate attacks for five days. One of the reasons we held them was because I had instant contact by radio with the guns, and the Japs never seemed to learn how to surprise us. They used to shout in English as they formed up, 'Give up!' which gave us warning each time an attack was coming in. One would judge just the right moment to call down gun- and mortar-fire to catch them as they were launching the attack, and every time they approached us they were decimated. They were not acting intelligently and did the same old stupid thing again and again.

We had experienced the Japs in the Arakan – we knew they bayoneted the wounded and prisoners and we didn't respect them. They had renounced any right to be regarded as human, and we thought of them as vermin to be exterminated. That was important. We were aroused and fought well. Also our backs were to the wall and we were going to sell our lives as expensively as we could. But we wondered how long we could hang on – not that we had any other option.

Throughout this period, we had no idea we were confronted by a whole Jap division and outnumbered by ten to one. '

Lieutenant Sam Horner
2nd Battalion, Royal Norfolk Regiment

'WE WERE ORDERED TO MARCH TO THE SOUTH OF KOHIMA TO CUT THE Imphal Road. This involved cutting a trail over a 7,000-foot ridge. The physical hammering we took is difficult to understand. The heat, humidity, altitude and the slope of almost every foot of ground combined to knock hell out of the stoutest. You gasp for air, which doesn't seem to come, you drag your legs upwards till they seem reduced to the strength of matchsticks, and all the time the sweat is pouring off you. Then you feel your heart pounding so violently you think it must burst its cage – it sounds as loud as a drum, even above the swearing and cursing going on around you. So you stop, horrified, to be prodded by the man behind you or cursed by an officer in front. '

The physical hammering we took is difficult to understand.

D-DAY – THE ALLIES INVADE

On the morning of 6 June 1944, more than 155,000 US, British and Canadian soldiers were ready to be shipped across the Channel to launch an Allied invasion of occupied France. D-Day had begun.

ABOVE: *Preparing for time off in France, men of the Royal Electrical and Mechanical Engineers swot up on what to expect.*

Planning for D-Day

The Allied invasion had taken years of top-level planning and organisation. Massive secrecy surrounded all elements of preparation for D-Day, from troop training and movement to the setting up of elaborate hoaxes to deceive the Germans. From 1943 a team worked to create the illusion of a huge Allied invasion force being organised in Kent. Dummy aircraft, tanks and landing craft were constructed from rubber and placed in strategic positions to trick German aircraft into believing that Allied troops were gathering to invade at Pas-de-Calais. As a result, on D-Day itself, the Germans had deployed many of their tanks and troops in the Calais area, rather than Normandy, where the real landings were taking place. By the time they realised their mistake, it was too late.

Lord Louis Mountbatten
Head of Combined Operations until October 1943

'In October 1941, I was recalled from Pearl Harbor to take up the job in charge of combined operations by Mr Winston Churchill. The very first day I reported to him, he said, 'You are to prepare the invasion of Europe for unless we can land and fight Hitler and beat his forces on land, we shall never win this war. You must devise and design the appliances, the landing craft and the technique to enable us to effect the landing against opposition and to maintain ourselves there. You must take the most brilliant officers to plan this great operation. You must take bases to use as training establishments where you can train the Navy, Army and Air Force to work as a single entity. The whole of the south coast of England is a bastion of defence against the invasion of Hitler. We've got to turn it into the springboard for our attack. There are three conditions necessary for a successful invasion. First, obviously, to get ashore against no matter what opposition. Secondly, having got ashore to stay ashore no matter what the weather conditions. Thirdly, to stop the enemy from building up his forces against you quicker than you can, otherwise he'll throw you back into the sea.'

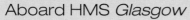
Lieutenant-Commander Cromwell Lloyd-Davies
Aboard HMS *Glasgow*

‘W E FOREGATHERED AT BELFAST, AND IMMEDIATELY WERE PUT UNDER complete security. No one was allowed ashore – no one was allowed on board. Then, for the first time, the operation orders were opened. These were very extensive and consisted of several sacks of orders. They also included a sort of rubber model of the whole of the Omaha Beach, which we were going to attack. It had been made in sections about a foot square. I understand that each section was made in a different part of the United States, so that they were never put together until they finally arrived in this country for D-Day. We assembled all of this in our hangar, and we were able then to sit down and look at the beach from a suitable distance. You saw the exact beach, including the background – as we would see it on the day. The security was intense, and even if a man went sick, he was sent to one special hospital in Belfast – which was under guard – and was not allowed to be removed. ’

You saw the exact beach, including the background – as we would see it on the day.

THE D-DAY INVASION

The invasion was time-critical – the tides had to be right and the weather calm enough for safe landings – but eventually, after one day's postponement, the massive armada set sail for Normandy on the night of 5 June. Eighteen thousand paratroops landed at dawn to capture essential bridges and disrupt German lines of communication, and the first US troops landed with tanks at Utah Beach at 6.30am. By midnight 155,000 Allied troops were ashore. Air support came in the form of RAF and American bombers who dropped bombs on targets in Northern France.

The success of the Calais deception meant that German troops had to be hurriedly sent to Normandy to bolster up the defence.

Yvonne Cormeau
Agent, F Section, SOE

‘ WE LISTENED TO THE RADIO FOR MESSAGES ALL THE TIME. THE MEN COULD not, of course. It fell to the people who were in the home – whether it was grandma or children – everyone contributed to try and listen in. The main times were the six and nine o'clock broadcasts from the BBC. One day we had a message, which said 'Listen in to the broadcasts twenty-four hours a day,' so the boss and I installed a little set in the hay up in a loft outside the farm, and we listened. We were told it might happen any time, 'You must listen in, you might hear your message. Get yourselves ready, put on the clothes you will wear for work when you go away and amke all arrangements for those who stay at home looking after the animals, that they have food.' Then finally the message came through that the armada had sailed, and there was terrific rejoicing, and a little crowd came up to our village during the night. We had been up all the time, cleaning what weapons we had. They had been hidden in the beehives. Then by morning, the others had turned up, and we allocated them to various people in the village we knew we could trust. ’

THE AIRBORNE INVASION

Staff Sergeant Roy Howard
Glider Pilot Regiment

‘ As A GLIDER PILOT, MY OBJECTIVE WAS A SMALL CORNER OF A particularly tiny field of rough pasture close to the Orne Bridge. If I overshot, I would crush us all against a 14-foot high embankment – if I undershot I would destroy my seven tons of powerless aircraft and its human cargo on a belt of 50-foot-high trees. There was simply no room for error. The significance of the two bridges to be attacked by a coup de main force was emphasised to us. With the 6th Airborne Division landing to the east of the river, and the whole invasion coming ashore to the west of the canal, it was vital that these troops should be able to cross the two bridges over the Orne and the canal. These two bridges were the only ones where you could do this between Caen and the sea. So it was absolutely vital that we had the maximum surprise element, and the only way to do this was for us to carry out our operation before the rest of the invasion started. So we were going to sneak in just after midnight, and some six-and-a-half hours before the seaborne invasion came ashore. ,

PARACHUTE LANDINGS

Corporal Dan Hartigan
1st Canadian Parachute Battalion

'HERE WE WERE, C COMPANY, JUST OVER 100 OF US, TAKING OFF IN LITTLE bombers to drop behind Hitler's 'impregnable Atlantic Wall' and take on Rommel's soldiers. We were perfectly aware that attacking infantry should have a three-to-one ratio in its favour, but according to intelligence reports we were going in to do our job at close on one-to-one. We were loaded to the hilt with grenades, Gammon bombs, flexible Bangalore torpedoes around our necks, two-inch mortar bombs, ammunition, weapons and water bottles. Our exposed skin was blackened with charcoal, the camouflage netting on our helmets was all tied up with burlap rags, and the space above the harnesses in our helmets was crammed with cigarettes or with plastic explosive. ,

We were loaded to the hilt with grenades, Gammon bombs, flexible Bangalore torpedoes around our necks, two-inch mortar bombs, ammunition, weapons and water bottles.

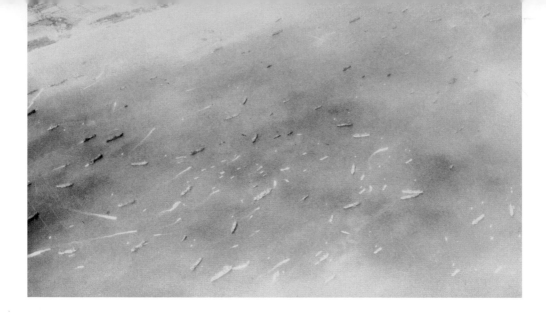

ABOVE: *An aerial view of thousands of Allied naval craft in the English Channel as seen from a US B-26 Martin Marauder on its way to participate in D-Day.*

THE SEA INVASION

Lieutenant-Commander Cromwell Lloyd-Davies
Aboard HMS *Glasgow*

"THE SCENE IN THE CHANNEL WAS QUITE AMAZING. IT WAS ALMOST LIKE Piccadilly Circus – there were so many ships there, and it was incredible to us that all this could be going on without the Germans knowing anything about it. But we never saw a German aircraft the whole time."

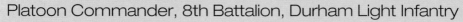

Lieutenant William Jalland
Platoon Commander, 8th Battalion, Durham Light Infantry

"THE PROW OF OUR BOAT WENT INTO THE SHINGLE AND THE AMERICAN sailor lowered the ramp and I knew exactly what I had to do. I was to walk off the gangway and on to the shingle and get off the beach quickly because a lot of shelling was expected. I went down, manfully I hope. I stepped off the ramp into the water. The water rushed over my head and I went straight to the bottom on my hands and knees. The prow was smashing into the shingle next to me and I watched it smashing against my legs and arms whenever it came near me. My waders were full of water and I couldn't get to the surface. I threw away the folding bicycle that I was carrying. Then I started to tear at the waders and I managed to get them off. I unfastened my webbing and slipped that off and eventually I landed on Hitler's Fortress Europe on my hands and knees, wet through, very frightened and completely unarmed. **'**

Signal Sergeant James Bellows
1st Battalion, Hampshire Regiment

' ALL ALONG THE BEACH, THERE WERE men lying dead and not JUST IN the waves. Some of them still had their tin hats on. A lot of them had been overridden by their landing craft as they came off. The landing craft became lighter as men came off and as it surged up the beach, any man that was in front went straight underneath. **'**

All along the beach, there were men lying dead and not just in the waves.

Sergeant William Spearman
No. 4 Commando

' THE PLANNERS MIGHT HAVE GONE THROUGH A LOT OF CAMPAIGNS AT A very high level but nobody can know what it's like to be on a beach where you can do nothing. Where you're under severe fire and you've got to get off. And it's only a person who's been through it a number of times who can know – you stay and die or you get off and live. People doing it for the first time – no matter how many times you tell them – they don't realise it. And people didn't get off the beach. They were so transfixed with fright, they couldn't get off. I was transfixed with fright but I had the certain knowledge that you either stopped and died or you got up and got away. So I took the coward's view and got out of the bloody place. **,**

Total Allied casualties on D-Day are estimated at 10,000, including 2,500 dead.

THE BATTLE OF NORMANDY

The Battle of Normandy is the name given to the fighting that took place between D-Day and the end of August 1944. After the Allies had broken through the coastal defences the Germans fought back with fierce counter attacks and it was weeks before the Allies could push further inland, meeting with stiff German resistance along the way.

Brigadier James Hill
3rd Parachute Brigade

6 IN THE DAYS FOLLOWING D-DAY, I EXPERIENCED SOME OF THE HARDEST fighting I had seen in the war. Involved were the 9th Parachute Battalion, 1st Canadian Parachute Battalion and 5th Battalion Black Watch. Imagine what it was like for a 9th Battalion soldier. These men had never seen a shot fired in anger until forty-eight hours before. Their average age was twenty. They had suffered an appalling night drop on D-Day. They had stormed the Merville battery and attacked Le Plein. They arrived on the ridge on the 7th June, 90 strong, having set off from England with over 600 officers and soldiers. They were minus their equipment and not exactly fresh. In the first eight days of the Battle of Normandy, my brigade, which started around 2,000 strong, lost about 50 officers and 1,000 other men. **,**

RIGHT: *The Paras prepare for D-Day and black up their faces to make a pre-dawn drop.*

Corporal Norman Habetin
Wireless Operator, 8th Battalion, Rifle Brigade Infantry

It was our first do and we had some very, very rude awakenings. It made all of us feel a lot sadder and a lot wiser, because we found out the enemy was a very real one and there was no question of a walkover or anything like that. We drove through Cheux, which was a bit of a mess. People all over the place had been killed. It was quiet, there were no guns firing. There was nothing in front of us except the Germans, but that didn't sink in because everything looked so normal – farmhouses, the sort of country we were used to. It was hard to believe that this was a front line.

Major Peter Martin
2nd Battalion, Cheshire Regiment

At first light, German tanks approached from the south and engaged the forward tanks of the Sherwood Foresters, knocking some of them out. The remainder withdrew to the reverse slope of Point 103, leaving my two platoons totally isolated.

The enemy tanks stood off about 120 yards away, hull down, and began shelling our bank with high explosive, causing casualties. On several occasions, when the Tigers cruised too far forward, with turrets open, our machine-gunners fired at them to make them close down. The situation was precarious, because if the enemy put in a determined attack from the south, he would be right on top of us before encountering our tanks or anti-tank guns. So we were very

> *'Oh God, please stop the shells. If you stop them, I'll be good for always.'*

cheered when soon after midday, recce parties from the 1st Dorsets arrived to say that Audrieu was being cleared and the Battalion would soon come to join us. At about that time, one of my platoons came up on the wireless and asked for help with evacuating a seriously wounded corporal. The only way was by jeep over an open field being shelled like fury. I thought I'd better drive the jeep myself so I told my driver to get out. To my disappointment, instead of saying, 'No sir! I will go with you!' he said, 'Right, sir,' and hopped out. I drove the jeep to a gap in the hedge of a field where the shells were bursting. I remember saying, 'Oh God, please stop the shells. If you stop them, I'll be good for always.' The shells promptly stopped and I got the corporal to safety. Many times during the war, I promised I would be a better person if I was allowed to survive. The promises never lasted very long.

Private Fritz Jeltsch
5th Company, 214 Regiment, German Army

AFTER NORMANDY WE CROSSED THE SEINE AT ROUEN AND CARRIED ON up towards Amiens and on the 31st August, when we'd made camp, one of our lookouts was so tired that he fell asleep at his post. He suddenly cried out and we looked up – and they were all there – the Free French and the Canadian troops. Of course we had to surrender then, because we were finished. There was no hope.

ARNHEM AND OPERATION MARKET GARDEN

Operation Market Garden was the Allied plan to seize five Rhine bridges in the Netherlands, over which Allied troops could advance into Germany, thereby bringing about a swift end to the war.

In the largest airborne operation in history, thousands of paratroopers were dropped behind enemy lines to take the five bridges in sequence – the last, at Arnhem, being assigned to the British 1st Airborne Division. Simultaneously, the British XXX Corps would drive through along a road linking the bridges and join the men at Arnhem. The first airborne landing was made in daylight on 17 September 1944 – and achieved a degree of surprise – but a second landing found the German defenders on the alert and casualties were heavy. The paratroopers desperately needed the support of ground troops to hold out at Arnhem, where German tanks were closing in, but strong enemy defences delayed the arrival of XXX Corps.

After more than a week of fighting, the final bridge at Arnhem was not taken and the Allies were defeated. Six thousand British paratroopers were taken prisoner and there were many thousands of casualties.

Lieutenant-Colonel John Frost
2nd Parachute Battalion

'TOWARDS EVENING, HEAVY TANKS APPEARED, INCREDIBLY MENACING and sinister in the half-light. Their guns swung from target to target, their shells bursting through our walls. Dust and debris was everywhere and the acrid smoke and smell of burning, combined with the intense noise, bemused us. But we had to stand our ground in order to meet any infantry advance.

Then our gunners brought a six-pounder round to the front and, combined with a bold move by the PIAT crews, we repelled their attack. Twenty yards behind us in the schoolhouse Major Hibbert, the brigade major, and the rest of the brigade staff had to sit it out, sniping whenever they had a chance.

The last onslaught had left us weary. Arnhem was burning. It was as daylight in the streets, a terrible enamelled, metallic daylight. However, that night was more peaceful. But at dawn the attack began again. This was our third day of holding on under continuous enemy pressure. It was all the more demanding on our patience in that it followed on after the exhilarating journey from England, our early successful thrust into Arnhem, and the high expectations of reinforcement from XXX Corps.

It was during this attack that I was wounded by mortar-fire – not badly, but extremely painfully, in both legs. After a time I was given morphia and taken down to the cellars. Freddie Gough assumed overall command at the bridge, but he used to come and refer any problems to me. We discussed doing a sortie and going northwards, but I felt it was much more important that we should stay in position, at the north end of the bridge, for as long as possible so as to give maximum help to anybody trying to cross from the south. So, even if we were left with no ammunition at all, we might have been able to do something to help them. There was, however, no way we could possibly move, we were absolutely sealed in by a ring of enemy infantry and armour.

ABOVE: *D-Day, 6 June 1944. British troops of the South Lancashire Regiment land on Sword Beach, backed up by amphibious tanks of the 13th/18th Hussars.*

RIGHT: *Normandy,*
26 June 1944. Armed
with Sten guns and
rifles with fixed
bayonets, British
infantrymen advance
tentatively in
Operation Epsom –
a drive to outflank
the city of Caen from
the west.

On the final evening the Brigade HQ caught fire, but there was no water. Jimmie Logan, my head doctor, came to see me and said, 'I'm afraid there is no hope of putting the flames out. Unless something else is done your 200 wounded are going to be burnt alive, including you, sir.' We'd almost ceased to be a fighting force because of lack of ammunition. The doctor then asked if he could try and make contact with the Germans so as to evacuate the wounded. The Germans agreed to a truce. Then everybody, including the SS, laboured with might and main, to get everybody out of the building, which by this time was blazing fiercely. After they'd got almost the last man out, the building collapsed. Then our men dug positions in back gardens, hoping to be able to continue resistance somehow, but when the morning came greatly superior numbers of German soldiers completely overwhelmed each group in turn. I was taken to St Elizabeth Hospital but I knew that as soon as possible the Germans would evacuate us further. I'd taken off my badges of rank and hoped that I would be able to escape as a private soldier, but early next morning we were put into ambulances and driven right into Germany. The Germans, and particularly the SS, were complimentary about the way we had fought the battle, but my bitterness was unassuaged. No enemy had beaten us before, and no body of men could have fought more courageously and tenaciously than the officers and men of the lst Parachute Brigade.

THE BATTLE OF THE BULGE, 1944–45

By mid-December the Allies had reached the forests of the Ardennes in northern France. Hitler ordered a desperate offensive and the suddenness of the assault put serious pressure on the thinly spread Allied (mostly American) forces who were defending 100 miles of front. Bad weather also meant that American fighter bombers were grounded at the start of the attack. On 23 December, however, the weather changed, the US 9th Air Force was able to join the attack and the Germans were repulsed. Hitler's best troops had been sacrificed, and there remained little strength with which to defend Germany. The Ardennes offensive was named 'The Battle of the Bulge' due to the 'bulge' created in the Allied line after the initial German attack.

ABOVE: *German infantry advancing during the Battle of the Bulge.*

Hans Behrens
9th Panzer Division

‘I REMEMBER CHRISTMAS – WE WERE AT OUR MOST WESTERLY POINT between Bastogne and St Hubert in the Ardennes. The turning point for me about the folly and the terror war instils, was that Bastogne was taken several times, to and fro, and one of those times we were coming down a hill and on the left side was a Sherman tank with its turret open. I don't know why, but I got out my vehicle and looked down inside in this tank. What I saw there was a young man absolutely charred black and one clean hole in the side of the turret. At that moment I realised that this man could be me and that he had a mother and a father. It became hard to carry on. ’

Major Jack Watson
13th Parachute Battalion

'OUR BATTALION RECEIVED AN ORDER TO MOVE TO PONDROME, TO ATTACK a village called Bure, and then secure another village, Grupont. These were the furthest points reached in the German offensive. My task was to attack Bure to secure the high ground. We were formed up ready to go in at 1300 hours. It was a bloody cold day, still snowing heavily, and even going through the wood to the start line was very difficult because the snow was as much as three or four feet deep in some places.

We looked down on this silent and peaceful village. The Germans knew we were there – they were waiting for us, and as soon as we started to break cover, I looked up and I could see about a foot above my head the branches of the trees being shattered by intense machine-gun fire and mortaring. They obviously had the guns on fixed lines and they pinned us down before we even got off the start line. This was the first time I'd led a company attack and within minutes I'd lost about one third of my men. [. . .]

We secured the first few houses, but it was difficult finding out just what was going on. I pulled in my platoon commanders to establish that they were secure and to start movement forward. It was eerie. We would be in one house, myself on the ground floor and my signalman telling me that there were Germans upstairs, and at other times they would be downstairs and we upstairs. It was a most unusual battle.

Our numbers were getting very depleted as we moved forward from house to house. I eventually got to the village crossroads by the old church, but by that time their 60-ton Tiger tanks had started to come in on us. It was the first time I had seen Tigers, and now here they were taking pot-shots, demolishing the houses. I moved from one side of the road to the other, deliberately drawing fire. A tank fired at me, and the next thing I knew the wall behind me was collapsing. But a PIAT team came running out, got within fifty yards of the tank, opened fire and smashed the tank's tracks. It went on like this all day – they counter-attacked but we managed to hold them.'

3

WAR COMES TO AN END

LEFT: *Jack Grundy comes home on leave and embraces his wife Dorothy, while his two children Randall and Gilda look on.*
ABOVE: *Parade celebrating the liberation of Paris.*

THE FALL OF GERMANY

As the Soviet army advanced toward Berlin, the Allies moved in from the west. Once in the heartland of Germany, they found a shattered landscape, with cities devastated by the Allied bombing raids.

ABOVE: *A shattered German tank, its turret torn off by anti-tank fire, showing the ferocity of the American defence of their positions at Bastogne, Ardennes.*

CROSSING THE RHINE

Germany now had little military strength with which to defend against the Allied invasion. Through February and March, Allied troops spread out along the length of the west bank of the river Rhine in preparation for massed crossings. On 7 March the Americans seized the bridge at Remagen. The US Third Army crossed the river to the south on 22–23 March, followed the next day by a British crossing to the north.

Sergeant Dan Hartigan
1st Canadian Parachute Battalion

'As we flew inland from the coast at about 1,200 feet I looked down to see a strange countryside. What I saw wasn't just a western European winter landscape, but ravaged terrain. The vegetation cover was so sparse and looked a somewhat burgundy tinge – mud oozing through turf. I'd never seen anything like it. It was quite surreal. For a few miles along the flight path and stretching towards the French coast on the Channel, as far as the eye could see, were hundreds of thousands of crater rings. There were so many it appeared almost incomprehensible. Yet there they were, sullen on the surface of this ravaged landscape. We had heard of no heavy-artillery attacks in this area, certainly nothing of this concentration of fury. Then it dawned on us quietly that we were flying over the World War I battlefields. It was a sobering sight, which filled us with melancholy for the suffering which must have gone on down there. Yet here we were 26 years after that last war ended, going to fight the same enemy. It took some time to come back to reality.'

Yet here we were 26 years after that last war ended, going to fight the same enemy.

'As we advanced through Germany, we arrived at Lübeck – which was an open city – about the last one to fall. Hundreds of Germans were handing themselves in to us because the Russians were on the other side and they chose us over them. They were coming in all sorts of vehicles to surrender – horses and carts – even a fire engine on one occasion. They were marching in and throwing their arms down. There were also released and escaped British ex-prisoners of war wandering around. As we were advancing, the Germans were marching them back and some were escaping or being left behind. They were flitting about, arming themselves and looking for their ex-guards to take some revenge. A lot of these chaps had been captured in 1940 and they didn't even recognise our uniforms. Once, when I'd left my tank and I was going back to my squadron, I turned round to see four chaps running towards me, waving their arms and hollering. They were RAF men who'd slipped out of a group that was being marched back from a prison camp. They'd climbed up to hide in the trees and they'd seen us arrive, but they couldn't recognise our uniforms so they spent hours trying to listen out for our voices to work out who we were.'

LEFT: *Hundreds of German prisoners of war in a compound after their units had been overrun in the Allied advance.*

DISCOVERING THE CONCENTRATION CAMPS

Hitler and the Nazis believed that certain groups of people were inferior and had no right to live. The chief target of the Nazis was the Jewish people, who were treated terribly throughout Germany and occupied Europe during the war years. From 1942 onwards, the Germans began transporting Jewish people from all over Europe to specially built sites, known as extermination camps. Millions of adults and children died in these places. Many were murdered – herded into huge gas chambers and gassed to death – while others were worked to death, starved or died of disease in the terrible conditions. This plan – to kill off an entire people – was called 'The Final Solution of the Jewish Problem' by the Nazis.

As the victorious Allies progressed through Germany, several of these camps were discovered.

RIGHT: *British soldiers supervise the distribution of food to inmates of the liberated Belsen concentration camp.*

Bombardier Martin Addington
Royal Artillery attached to Marine Commando

6 THERE WAS AN UTTER SILENCE WHEN WE WENT IN AND SAW THESE POOR creatures crawling about and scratching. Those who had the strength ran up to you asking for food or a cigarette, with flea-bitten rags on them. They were like, if you can imagine, a skeleton with a bit of skin on, that's all. They were all ages – men, women, kids. We couldn't speak to them. We were too choked to speak. 9

ABOVE: *A general view of Flossenburg concentration camp showing the barracks and electrified fencing.*

Sergeant Alan Brewster
58th Light Anti-Aircraft Regiment, Royal Artillery

'WE CAME UP TO THESE MARVELLOUS WROUGHT-IRON GATES, WHICH THE Germans opened for us to let us in. I think they'd been disarmed by now, they didn't have any rifles, and we drove in and these inmates, all in their striped uniforms, looked up at us. They were lying around on the ground. They had terrible sunken eyes and they put their hands out to try and touch us as we went past. It was a complete shock to us. We didn't have the faintest idea.

I walked to the main building and I heard this thudding noise. I recognised it from my days in a band. It was someone putting a bass drum on the ground. I wondered where the devil it was coming from. I kept on walking and I came across all these men in their striped uniforms, lined up in front of the main

They had terrible sunken eyes and they put their hands out to try and touch us as we went past.

building with musical instruments and they started playing 'God Save the King'. I stood stiffly to attention. Some of the inmates who were lying dying on the ground struggled to their feet, they were helping each other up and they stood to attention too. And then a couple of the inmates who were in better health ran amongst the others, taking off their caps. It was an amazing sight. At the end of the anthem, they slowly sank down to the ground again. **'**

Clare Parker
Inmate, Mauthausen concentration camp

' FOR US, LIBERATION WAS JUST THESE AMERICAN SOLDIERS WHO HAD NO food on them, who found us accidentally. They were driving past and they saw these people through the gate.
As they had nothing on them, they didn't know what to do, you know. The only thing they had on them was cigarettes and so they gave us each a cigarette and we tried to eat them, I didn't know what they were. I was a child – I just didn't know. **'**

RIGHT: *At Belsen, a British soldier talks to English-born Louis Bonerguer, who was captured and interned after parachuting into Germany to work under cover in 1941.*

The End of War in Europe

On 2 May 1945, two days after Hitler's suicide, the city of Berlin surrendered to the Soviet army. On 7 May, the Germans surrendered unconditionally in the presence of senior officers from Britain, America, the Soviet Union and France. The Allies celebrated their victory on the following day – VE (Victory in Europe) Day. In London, Winston Churchill announced the news over the radio.

LEFT: *Russian soldiers saluting on the balcony of the Chancellery after the fall of Berlin.*

Sergeant George Teal
Tank Commander, Coldstream Guards

'AS SOON AS THE ARMISTICE WAS SIGNED, THOUSANDS OF GERMAN soldiers appeared, lining the roads. Our officer said, 'Keep your guns loaded and your fingers on the trigger. First sign of trouble, we'll mow the bastards down.' We were itchy-fingered because there was so many of them. At Cuxhaven Airfield, we had to take the surrender of the German 6th Parachute Regiment and they came marching in, wearing brand-new uniforms with flags flying, swords out. Someone wanted to present arms to them but our CO, Colonel

RIGHT: *British and Russian troops in the garden of the former Reichs Chancellery. The entrance to Hitler's bunker is immediately behind them.*

Gooch, wouldn't allow it. They halted and their commanding officer came forward and handed over his sword and put his hand out. Colonel Gooch said, 'This has not been a football match,' and refused to shake hands.

> *Colonel Gooch said, 'This has not been a football match,' and refused to shake hands.*

Ellen Harris
Reuters reporter in Parliament

I SHALL NEVER FORGET IT. I COULDN'T MOVE – I COULDN'T DO anything, whatever had happened. Although we'd known this was coming, the House of Commons itself just went into one great roar of cheers, papers went up in the air, I just sat and the tears were rolling down – it was relief after all this long time. And this kept up, the roaring and cheering and shouting for some time.

Lilias Walker
Teenager in Hull

'I REMEMBER THE ANNOUNCEMENT BEING MADE ON THE RADIO THAT, AT such and such a time, the war would be over. Where people had got stuff from I don't know where, but immediately there were bonfires and everybody drew back their curtains and turned on all their lights. Every single light in the house was on because, of course, no lights had been allowed during the war.'

Every single light in the house was on because, of course, no lights had been allowed during the war.

Peter Bennett
Child in Godalming

'WE HAD VE DAY PARTIES ON THE VILLAGE GREEN – BONFIRES AND LATER on, the following year, we got a letter from King George VI – thanking the boys and girls for coping so well during the war and reminding us what our older brothers and sisters had done for us – which was a nice thought. I remember having oranges during VE parties – but I was sick after eating the orange peel, having no idea that wasn't what you did. '

ABOVE: *Big Ben and the Palace of Westminster floodlit as part of the VE Day celebrations.*

THE ATOMIC BOMB

It had taken years of research and development to create the world's first nuclear weapon – the atomic bomb. When the order was given to drop the bomb on Japan, it unleashed total devastation.

ABOVE: *The mushroom cloud from the atomic bomb dropped on Nagasaki.*

The End of War in the Far East

While the war in Europe had ended in May 1945, fighting in the Far East went on for another three months. As the Americans fought from island to island in the Pacific and launched bombing raids on Japanese cities, plans were made to invade Japan. However, American casualties on the islands of Iwo Jima and Okinawa had been heavy, and a prolonged campaign would only add to this toll. Seeing Japan under pressure in Burma, China and at home, President Truman decided to try to end the war with one mighty blow.

On 6 August, the American B-29 bomber, *Enola Gay*, dropped an atomic bomb, the first ever used, on the city of Hiroshima. It devastated a huge area and left an estimated 66,000 Japanese people dead and 69,000 gravely injured. On 9 August a second bomb was dropped on Nagasaki, where a similar number perished. Reeling from the second attack, Japan surrendered on 14 August. The Second World War was over.

ABOVE: *A Japanese private surrendering to British soldiers.*

Geoffrey Sherring
Radio operator with Merchant Navy, POW in Nagasaki

‘I WAS WORKING WITH AN AUSTRALIAN WHOSE NAME WAS Bernard O'Keefe. I said to him, 'There's nobody about – let's nip in there and have a smoke.' This we did, and it must have been a couple of minutes to eleven. I had a burning glass, and we each had a cigarette end somewhere about us, so we set alight our cigarettes with the sunlight, and retreated back into the trench, which was roofed, to smoke in peace. The atomic bomb went off whilst we were in there. Bernie said to me, 'I can hear a car on the road.' I said, 'Don't be ridiculous – there's no petrol in Japan, let alone cars – it must be an aeroplane.' He said, 'I'm going out to have a look.'

He began crawling away from me towards the hole in the roof of the trench that he could get out of. As he did so, and I was looking after him, I saw the flash from the bomb – which was exactly like the sort of bluish light that you get from an electrical welding operation. It was very blue, and it came in exactly the opposite direction from the sun's rays – it completely eclipsed them. It was this thin, blue blazing light, shining down a square hole in front of Bernie, who hadn't, fortunately, reached the hole – or he would have been burned too. Then we heard the vibration and shaking, which wasn't a bang by any means. It was a continuous shaking of the whole air and earth about it. It was separated by several seconds from the flash, because we were not directly underneath the bomb – we were about 1,100 yards away.

Then this thundering, rolling, shaking came along, and everywhere went completely dark. What had happened was the shock wave had rolled over us,

Then this thundering, rolling, shaking came along, and everywhere went completely dark.

lifting as it went, all the earth and dust around us and blowing the building flat at the same time. So when we came out, in a matter of seconds, we came out into a choking brown fog. This fog lasted for quite a while before the south-westerly breeze blew it back up the city. As it did so, we had a shower of most peculiar rain. It was in very, very large droplets, about as big as grapes, and it was almost entirely mud – just thick blobs of mud falling from the sky.

It didn't take us long to realise that there was something seriously amiss, because the camp had collapsed and there wasn't a building standing anywhere near us. We could see further than we'd ever seen before across the city, which was all in a heap. Most of the buildings had been made of wood and some of them nearer to the site of the bomb had already been set on fire and it was spreading. I ran to a storehouse nearby and the Japanese in charge of this must have been standing in the doorway, because his skin was completely burnt off him, and he had fallen on the ground. He was a distressing sight, with a lot of his insides hanging out. I was trying to make him comfortable but all the skin came off his arms on to my hands, just like thin wet rubber. He, of course, was in great pain, and shouting for a stretcher – which I couldn't provide for him so I left him.

On a horse and cart we made our way out of the town in a westward direction, up into the hills. By early to mid-afternoon, we had made ourselves as comfortable as we could on a terrace overlooking the city, and thought we should stay there for a while. But the houses, each of which was on its own terrace, had begun to burn from the bottom upwards. We exhorted the Japanese who lived in the house on the end of the terrace we were sitting on to move their stuff before their house was burnt down. Nothing would induce them to go. Absolutely nothing.

I said, 'Come on lads – we've got to do something.' So we all dashed into this house and collected everything we could take out – for instance drawers with all their contents – and passed them from hand to hand out on to the field. The Japanese were pitifully grateful about this, but they would never go in to help themselves. I got the feeling they felt this was almost a supernatural occurrence, and that they couldn't do anything about it.

I said, 'Come on lads – we've got to do something.'

We were feeling very tired from our exertions and hoping nothing more would happen, when a Japanese soldier came along. He had his rifle and still had his bayonet fixed. He told us that the bulk of our prisoners were on the opposite side of the city – over on the other side, occupying a similar hillside position to ourselves. He pointed out that they had no stores, food or blankets – nothing. I was very impressed by the way he went about his duties in the middle of all this terrible chaos, so I got three Dutch East India men and we put buckets on thick bamboo poles, and we loaded these up with tinned food of various kinds and we folded blankets on to the poles, and carrying these burdens, we set off into the burning city. '

RIGHT: *Survivors wander through the devastated landscape of Nagasaki.*

THE WAR IS OVER

After the widespread joy of VE and VJ days, there was for many a sense of anticlimax. The post-war world to which they had returned was very different from the one which they had left.

ABOVE: *A street party in Stepney, East London to celebrate VE Day.*

ABOVE: *Eager soldiers pulling copies of the* London Times *off the press to read about the news of Germany's surrender on 7 May 1945.*

Sergeant Clifford Bailey
Rifle Brigade, released prisoner of the Japanese

'AFTER I GOT BACK TO ENGLAND, I WENT HOME. I ARRIVED AT MY HOUSE and I walked in, and it was quite an emotional experience, actually, because I'd been away since '41. My father had been reasonably fit when I left – now he was virtually bedridden with a chronic heart condition. He was being looked after by a cousin of mine who had made her home with us through the war, because my mother had died in 1940. She greeted me at the door – very emotional. She said, 'Oh, you know, be careful of your father – not too much shock.' She said, 'He's been very ill.' One of the rooms had been converted into a bedsitting room for him, because he couldn't go up the stairs. And I went in, and he greeted me calmly. He looked at me – he said, 'I knew you'd come back.' We talked well into the early hours of the morning, and eventually, about three o'clock in the morning I suppose, I went to bed.

That was quite an experience, because up to that time, I'd been with a crowd of people, so I'd never been completely on my own. To go into that bedroom and close the door . . . all the thoughts came flooding back then, you know, the preceding years. It was the first time you could stop and really come to terms with yourself and find out what it was all about.

He looked at me – he said, 'I knew you'd come back.'

ABOVE: *Children returning home, wave goodbye from the rear window of their bus to the families with whom they were billeted as evacuees.*

Sylvia Taylor
Child in Hook, Surrey

❝ AFTER THE WAR, EVERYONE WAS SO VERY HAPPY, ELATED AND RELIEVED. We didn't know what was coming because we didn't remember what was before the war. We thought we would have sweets, heating and coal. ❞

RIGHT: *A house decorated with flags and banners to celebrate the liberation of Guernsey.*

Major Corrie Halliday
11th Hussars

❝ AFTER THE WAR THERE WERE TIMES WHEN I WAS SO DEPRESSED THAT I came close to suicide. It wasn't so much that I was fed up with having survived the war or that I felt bad that some of my friends had been killed and I hadn't. It was the future. I'd had six years taken away from me. Whereas before the war there was a future – if I didn't like the bank I was working in at the time then I was free to change direction, but by the end of the war I'd got round to asking what good has the last six years done me? Why am I here? Where am I going from here? ❞

Corporal Jack Sharpe
1st Battalion, Leicestershire Regiment, prisoner of war

'In the end I was the longest survivor in that jail. During that time I got scurvy, which made my eyes like balls of fire, all matter coming out. My mouth was all swollen and red raw. I could barely swallow. Then I got scabies, which killed so many. I was covered in scabs from head to foot. There was no treatment. Mother Nature or death took over. I kept saying, 'Keep going, keep going,' and months later the scabs disappeared. So many around me were starving to death or simply giving up.

The only time I faltered was when my best friend died. I couldn't see the sense in going on. But I had to. In May 1945 we heard about the end of the war in Europe so I was determined to stay alive. Then in August the American bombers arrived and blasted Singapore. Two days after the raid the Japs surrendered.

When the camp was relieved the lads picked me up like a conquering hero. As I was being carried out I saw the sign over the gate and I asked the lads to put me down. I was determined to walk for freedom. I managed a few steps, got outside and then the lads had to pick me up again. I had weighed eleven stone when I was captured – I was now only four.

I'd contracted dysentery and was unconscious for 48 hours in Changi. When I came round I saw the padre so I thought I was in heaven. Later, a really thoughtful NCO came into the ward and called me outside to sit on the verandah. He gave me 38 letters, all from my mother. She had never believed I was dead and had written to me every month for more than three years. Reading them I just wept and wept. I thought of my dear mother and all the pain she had been through. That was the first time I'd allowed myself to cry. After a few weeks' rest I was flown to Bangalore to recover.

One day in Bangalore, I was sitting on my bed and feeling a bit low – and heard footsteps. I looked up and there was my older brother, Jess. I'd made him promise to stay home and look after our mother, but he had joined up. Now he had got special extended leave to come to find me. He stayed with me and taught me to walk again as he had done when I was a child. All the same, it was a year before I was fit enough to go back to England. There at long last I saw my mother.

Corporal Patricia Coulson
RAF, administration

'After the men came back from the Far East, they were given their Post Office books. We received a letter from a mother. Briefly, it read, 'My son who is living with me, has been given his Post Office book. Could you please give me authority to draw out the money to look after him? He has returned minus his arms and legs.' He was 23 years old. This sums it all up. However much I may not remember of the past as I grow older, these things I saw and heard during this period of my life will always be with me.'

ABOVE: *A British soldier gives a helping hand to an old lady in the desolated city of Caen.*

Second World War Timeline

This timeline shows some of the key events of the Second World War.

1939
13 March – 30 November

15 March
Germany occupies Czechoslovakia.

22 May
Germany and Italy sign the 'Pact of Steel' and become allies.

23 August
Germany and the Soviet Union sign the Non-Aggression Pact, stating that neither side will attack one another under any circumstance.

1 September
Germany invades Poland. Children are evacuated from major British cities.

3 September
Britain and France declare war on Germany.

17 September
The Soviet Union invades Poland.

27 September
The Polish capital, Warsaw, surrenders to Germany.

29 September
Germany and the Soviet Union make an agreement to divide Poland between them.

30 November
The Soviet Union invades Finland.

1940
8 April – 9 December

9 April
German troops invade Denmark and Norway.

10 May
Germans begin invasion of Holland, Belgium and Luxembourg using 'Blitzkrieg' tactics.

10 May
Winston Churchill is appointed British Prime Minister.

28 May – 4 June
A mass evacuation of retreating Allied forces takes place at Dunkirk, France.

11 June
Italy begins bombing of Malta.

14 June
German troops enter Paris.

22 June
France signs an armistice with Germany. Italy joins the war.

10 July – 31 October
The Luftwaffe and the RAF clash in the Battle of Britain.

11 August
Italy invades British Somaliland.

7 September
The Blitz begins as the Luftwaffe start heavy bombing raids on British cities.

17 September
Italy invades Egypt.

22 September
Japan occupies Indochina.

27 September
Germany, Italy and Japan sign the Tripartite (Axis) Pact and become allies.

9 December
British soldiers attack Italian forces in the Western Desert.

1941
22 January – 25 December

22 January
British and Australian forces capture Tobruk, Libya.

1 March
Bulgaria joins the Axis powers.

6 April
Germany invades Yugoslavia and Greece.

27 May
The Royal Navy sink the German warship *Bismarck*.

22 June
Germany begins *Operation Barbarossa*, the invasion of the Soviet Union.

8 September
The siege of Leningrad (St Petersburg) begins.

7 December
Japan bombs the American fleet at Pearl Harbor and the USA enters the war.

11 December
Germany and Italy declare war on the USA.

25 December
Hong Kong surrenders to the Japanese.

1942
2 January - 11 November

2 January
The Japanese capture Manila, the capital of the Philippines.

26 January
First American forces arrive in the United Kingdom.

15 February
Singapore falls to the Japanese and approximately 60,000 prisoners are taken.

30 March
The first trainloads of Jewish people arrive at Auschwitz-Birkenau extermination camp.

1 May
Japanese capture Mandalay, Burma.

4 June
The US fleet defeats the Japanese in the Pacific in the Battle of Midway.

21 June
Rommel's Afrika Korps recaptures Tobruk, Libya.

1 September
Germans driven back in the Battle of Alam Halfa.

12 September
The battle for Stalingrad begins.

23 October – 3 November
Allied and German forces fight the second Battle of El Alamein. The Germans are defeated.

11 November
Germans and Italians occupy Vichy, France.

1943
2/3 January - 13 October

2/3 January
Soviet troops begin recapture of the Caucasus region of the Soviet Union.

23 January
The Eighth Army under Montgomery takes Tripoli.

2 February
The Germans surrender at Stalingrad, their first major defeat.

25 February
British and American military aircraft begin round-the-clock bombing raids on Germany.

10 - 16 March
The Battle of the Atlantic reaches its peak when 21 Allied ships are sunk by German U-boats.

12 May
German and Italian troops surrender in North Africa.

9/10 July
The Allies land in Sicily.

25 July
The Italian leader, Mussolini, is overthrown.

8 September
Italian armistice is announced.

9 September
Allied landings at Salerno and Taranto, Italy.

13 October
Italy declares war on Germany.

1944
6 January - 26 October

6 January
Soviet troops advance into Poland.

22 January
Allies land at Anzio, Italy.

27 January
The siege of Leningrad ends after 900 days.

22 March
Japanese forces begin their attempted invasion of India.

18 May
Allied troops take Monte Cassino, Italy.

4 June
Allies capture Rome.

6 June
D-Day. Allied forces invade France, landing on the beaches of Normandy.

25 August
Paris is liberated by the Allies.

11 September
Allied troops enter Nazi Germany.

26 September
Allied troops are forced to withdraw from Arnhem.

6 October
The Soviet army enters Czechoslovakia.

20 October
US troops land in the Philippines.

23-26 October
Americans and Japanese fight the Battle of Leyte Gulf in the Philippines, the largest naval battle in history.

30 April
Hitler commits suicide.

4 May
German forces in North-west Europe surrender to Montgomery.

7 May
Germany surrenders. The Battle of the Atlantic finally ends.

8 May
VE (Victory in Europe) day.

6 August
The US drops the first atomic bomb on Hiroshima, Japan.

9 August
A second atomic bomb is dropped on Nagasaki, Japan.

14 August
Japan surrenders.

15 August
VJ (Victory in Japan) Day.

1945
3 January - 15 August

SECOND WORLD WAR STATISTICS

3 January
British army begin new offensive in Burma.

17 January
Warsaw is liberated by the Soviets.

13/14 February
German city of Dresden is bombed by the Allies.

19 February
US troops land on Japanese island of Iwo Jima.

24 February
US troops capture Manila, capital of the Philippines.

20 March
British and Indian troops capture Mandalay, Burma.

22 March
US and British forces begin to cross the River Rhine, Germany.

29 March
Soviets enter Austria.

11 April
Buchenwald concentration camp is liberated by the Allies.

15 April
Belsen concentration camp is liberated by the Allies.

The Second World War was the deadliest conflict in history. No-one knows exactly how many people were killed in the war but it is thought to be approximately 55 million people. It is known that there were more civilian deaths than military deaths.

British Military Ranks During The Second World War

The list begins with the highest military rank and goes down, rank by rank, to the lowest.

ARMY	NAVAL RANKS	AIR FORCE
FIELD MARSHAL	ADMIRAL OF THE FLEET	MARSHAL OF THE RAF
GENERAL	ADMIRAL	AIR CHIEF MARSHAL
LIEUTENANT-GENERAL	VICE-ADMIRAL	AIR MARSHAL
MAJOR-GENERAL	REAR-ADMIRAL	AIR VICE-MARSHAL
BRIGADIER-GENERAL	COMMODORE	AIR COMMODORE
COLONEL	CAPTAIN	GROUP CAPTAIN
LIEUTENANT-COLONEL	COMMANDER	WING COMMANDER
MAJOR	LIEUTENANT-COMMANDER	SQUADRON LEADER
CAPTAIN	LIEUTENANT	FLIGHT LIEUTENANT
LIEUTENANT	SUB-LIEUTENANT	FLYING OFFICER
2ND LIEUTENANT	ACTING SUB-LIEUTENANT/ENSIGN	PILOT OFFICER
SERGEANT-MAJOR	MIDSHIPMAN	ACTING PILOT OFFICER
SERGEANT		
CORPORAL		
LANCE-CORPORAL		
PRIVATE		

Picture Credits

GLOSSARY

AFRIKA KORPS German forces which fought in North Africa

AIRCRAFT CARRIER a warship equipped with a large deck for the taking off and landing of warplanes

AIR RAID a bombing attack carried out from the air

ALLIES the alliance of countries, including Great Britain, France, the USA, China and the Soviet Union, who fought the Axis powers during the war

AMMUNITION supplies of bullets and shells

ANTI-AIRCRAFT GUN a gun designed to fire at enemy aircraft

ARMADA a fleet of warships

ARMISTICE an agreement to stop fighting

ARP stands for Air Raid Precautions, an organisation staffed by local people during the war to help the community before, during and after air raids

ARTILLERY heavy guns that cannot be held, such as cannons, also the name for the military units that use them e.g. Royal Artillery

ARYAN used by the Nazis to describe the blond-haired, blue-eyed racial ideal of Nazi Germany

ASSAULT a sudden violent attack

ATOMIC BOMB an extremely destructive bomb whose explosive power results from the sudden release of energy from nuclear fission

AXIS the defeated powers in the war: Germany, Italy, Japan, Romania and the countries that fought with them

BANGALORE TORPEDO an explosive placed on the end of a long extendable tube, used to clear obstacles from a distance

BARRAGE concentrated artillery bombardment

BATMAN a soldier assigned to an officer as a servant

BATTALION a unit of roughly 850 soldiers, forms part of a regiment

BATTERY the place where the artillery is positioned

BAYONET a long sharp metal blade attached to a rifle

BEF stands for British Expeditionary Force, an army that was created in 1939 specifically to be sent to France in the event of war with Germany

BILLETING making householders provide a room for evacuees or essential war workers

BLACKOUT to conceal all visible lights in a city as a precaution against air raids

BLITZ Germany's bombing of British cities that began in September 1940

BLITZKRIEG meaning 'lightning war', the German army's fast advance through Europe in 1939–40

BOYES ANTI-TANK RIFLE a large heavy British rifle designed to penetrate the armour of enemy tanks

BREN GUN a light machine gun used by British troops during the war

BUGLER a soldier who plays the bugle (a type of trumpet) as a military signal

BULLY BEEF canned beef, a common meal for soldiers during the war

BURLAP coarse fabric

CAMOUFLAGE to blend in with the background

CARLEY FLOAT a sturdy life raft made from copper, cork and canvas

CHINDIT special forces who fought behind the Japanese lines in Burma

CIVILIAN a person who is not a soldier

CO stands for Commissioned Officer or Commanding Officer

COMMUNISM a form of government that aims to create a classless society with no ownership of private property

CONCENTRATION CAMP a prison camp for non-military prisoners

CONSCRIPTION a law that states men of certain ages must do military service

CONVOY a group of ships or other vehicles travelling together

CRATER a hole or pit in the ground where a bomb, shell, or mine has exploded

CSM stands for Company Sergeant Major

D-DAY 6 June 1944, the day the Allies landed in Normandy to free Europe from Nazi occupation

DEMOCRACY government by the people through their elected representatives

DIVE BOMBER a fighter plane that drops its bombs while diving at the enemy

DOGFIGHT an aerial battle that takes place between two or more aircraft

DUGOUT a pit dug into the ground and used as a shelter

EASTERN FRONT the part of Eastern Europe where Germany fought against the Soviet Union

E-BOAT a small fast German torpedo boat

ENLIST to enrol in the army willingly

EVACUATE to move people away from a place of danger

EVACUEE a person who has been moved from a place of danger

FASCISM a form of government that crushes any political opposition with state power and which favours extreme nationalism and military force

FINAL SOLUTION the Nazi plan to systematically kill all the Jewish people in Europe

FLAK anti-aircraft guns or shells

FLANK the left or right side of an army

FRONT LINE the line of confrontation between troops in a war

GAMMON BOMB a small British hand grenade

GLIDER a small engineless aircraft used in the war to transport troops for aerial invasions

HANGAR a enclosed building that holds aircraft

HOLOCAUST the mass murder of millions of Jews and others by the Nazis during the war

HQ stands for headquarters, the place where operations are directed from

INFANTRY foot soldiers

INTELLIGENCE in military terms, information gained about the enemy, also used to describe the agents that gather the information

IRVINE JACKET a flight jacket worn by British air-crew

'JAP' slang word for a Japanese soldier

'JERRY' slang word for a German soldier

KAISER the Emperor of Germany during the First World War

'KING'S SHILLING' the expression 'taking the King's shilling' refers to the payment a new army recruit receives when they join up

KNOT a unit of speed used by ships and boats

KUKRI a large knife with a heavy curved blade used by Gurkhas

LATRINE a toilet in a camp or barracks

LUFTWAFFE the German air force

'MAE WEST' slang word for 'vest', used to describe a life jacket

MAGINOT LINE a sophisticated series of fortifications built to protect France's frontier with Germany

MAHJONG a Chinese game played by four people

MISTRAL a cold, dry northerly wind common in Southern France

MMG stands for motor machine gun

MORTAR a large metal tube that is used to fire an explosive mortar bomb at a target

MORTAR PIT a hole in which the operator stands to fire the mortar

NAZI short for 'National Socialist', the ruling political party led by Adolf Hitler in Germany during the war years

OCCUPATION when a state, country or territory is forcibly taken over by another

OFFENSIVE an attack or assault

PACT an agreement or treaty

PADRE means 'father', used to address a priest or member of the clergy

PARATROOPER a specially trained soldier who parachutes behind the enemy line

PHOSPHOROUS BOMB a chemical bomb which caused terrible burns on explosion

PIAT TEAM a team of British soldiers operating an anti-tank weapon, stands for Projector, Infantry, Anti Tank

PLATOON a military unit that consists of two or more sections and a headquarters

PORT the left hand side of a ship or aircraft

POW stands for 'prisoner of war', a person captured by the enemy during wartime

RAF the British Royal Air Force

RECCE slang word for 'reconnaissance', exploring an area to gather information

REFUGEE a person forced to leave their country for reasons of safety

RESISTANCE an organisation in an occupied country whose members secretly work to fight the occupying force

RUDDER a steering mechanism on a boat or plane

SCABBARD a long thin cover for the blade of a sword

'SCRAMBLE' used by pilots to describe taking off as quickly as possible to intercept enemy planes

SEA BOOTS rubber boots for wearing on boats and ships

SENTRY a guard

SHELL an explosive that is fired by an artillery gun

SHERMAN TANK an American tank used by the Allies in the war

SHRAPNEL fragments of an exploded bomb, mine or shell

SLIT TRENCH a narrow ditch dug in the ground to protect one soldier or a small group

SOE stands for Special Operations Executive, an intelligence organisation set up during the war to train secret agents to work behind enemy lines

SORTIE a military action in which besieged troops move swiftly out from their position to attack the enemy

SOVIET UNION also known as the USSR (Union of Soviet Socialist Republics), a huge Communist country that included Russia and which lasted until the early 1990s

SQUADRON a unit of ten to eighteen military planes

STARBOARD the right hand side of a ship or aircraft

STEN GUN a light submachine gun used by the British

STERN the rear of a ship or boat

STRAFE from the German *strafen* (to punish), used to describe machine gun fire from low flying enemy aircraft

STUKA a German dive bomber aircraft, hence the term to be 'stuka-ed'

TIGER TANK name given to a type of German tank

'TOMMY' slang word for a British soldier

TORPEDO an underwater missile that is fired from a boat or submarine

TURRET a revolving weapon platform on top of a tank

U-BOAT a German submarine

UNCONDITIONAL SURRENDER when a country surrenders and accepts all conditions imposed by the victors

USAAF stands for United States Army Air Force

VE stands for 'Victory in Europe'

VICKERS a large machine gun used by the British army

VICKERS POM POM slang expression describing the noise of a .05 heavy machine gun

VJ stands for 'Victory in Japan'

WAAF stands for Women's Auxiliary Air Force, formed during the war so that women could work as part of the Royal Air Force

WESTERN FRONT the area in Western Europe where the Axis powers confronted the Allies

Finding out more about The Second World War

If you are interested in finding out more about the Second World War, there is a huge amount of material available. Your local or school library should have a range of books that will tell you about different aspects of the war. Many films, documentaries and television series have been made on this subject over the years and you may be able to borrow these from the library on video or DVD. Some of the well-known classic films are *The Dambusters* (1954), *The Bridge on the River Kwai* (1957), *The Longest Day* (1962), *The Great Escape* (1963) and *A Bridge Too Far* (1977), but there are numerous others. *The World at War* is probably the best known factual series about the war.

Many towns and cities have local museums, some of which will have information about the effects of the war in your area. You may be able to find some interesting accounts and photographs of what life was like during the war, particularly during the Blitz. You may even have relatives who actually lived through the war and who are able to tell you their own stories.

There are many hundreds of eyewitness accounts from the Second World War. A wonderfully varied selection of these accounts can be found in the book and the CD: *Forgotten Voices of the Second World War* by Max Arthur, the source for the stories contained in this edition.

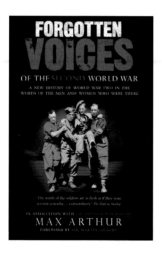

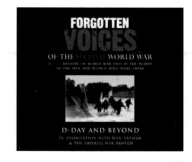

The Internet contains a wealth of information about the war.
Here are some good websites to browse:

www.bbc.co.uk/history/war/wwtwo/
www.spartacus.schoolnet.co.uk/2WW.htm
www.historylearningsite.co.uk
http://www.worldwar-2.net/
www.channel4.com/history/microsites/H/history/browse/britain-ww2.html

ABOUT THE IMPERIAL WAR MUSEUM

IMPERIAL WAR MUSEUM LONDON

Packed with fascinating exhibits and amazing facts, this museum tells the story of what life was like in the front line and on the home front during both World Wars. Visitors can experience the drama of an air raid, complete with sounds, smells and special effects, find out about evacuees and rationing, and discover the undercover world of wartime espionage.

CHURCHILL MUSEUM AND CABINET WAR ROOMS

Concealed beneath the streets of Westminster, the Cabinet War Rooms was Winston Churchill's secret underground headquarters during the Second World War. Visitors can see where Churchill worked, ate and slept, protected from the bombing raids above, and discover more about the life of this extraordinary man in the Churchill Museum.

HMS BELFAST

The museum's third London branch is a Second World War ship moored on the River Thames near the Tower of London. It gives a unique insight into naval history and the harsh, dangerous conditions which her crew endured. Visitors can explore nine decks to find out what life was like when living and working on board a warship.

IMPERIAL WAR MUSEUM DUXFORD

Based near Cambridge, this is one of the country's biggest air museums, sited on a former Battle of Britain station. It has a unique collection including bi-planes, Spitfires, Concorde and Gulf War jets. During the summer, many of these legendary aircraft take to the sky for Duxford's world-class airshows.

IMPERIAL WAR MUSEUM NORTH

The Museum's newest branch in Manchester is housed in an unusual and dramatic building representing conflict on land, sea and air. This Museum offers exhibitions, family events and a dynamic audio-visual show called the Big Picture.

All sorts of interactive family activities take place throughout the year at every branch of the Imperial War Museum. These range from code-breaking activities to art and sculpture sessions and the chance to handle wartime artefacts as well as opportunities to meet veterans and find out first-hand what life was like during wartime.

For further information about the Imperial War Museum visit:
www.iwm.org.uk

INDEX OF CONTRIBUTORS

INDEX